60 MINUTE CFO

BRIDGING THE GAP BETWEEN BUSINESS OWNER, BANKER AND CPA

DAVID A. DURYEE

I dedicate this book to the owners and managers of closely held businesses whose energy, determination, creativity, and hard work help keep our economy healthy and vibrant. I hope this book provides you with some of the tools needed to achieve continued success and profitability.

David A. Duryee
2021

READER REVIEWS

Duryee explains the financial management side of a business in a very clear and understandable manner. This book is what every successful business leader must know and understand how to run a business successfully. **Brandt Allen, DBA, Professor Emeritus, Darden School of Business, University of Virginia.**

This is a great book! When the CEO and leadership team understand the numbers and what they mean, they have a decided advantage. Duryee's book is perfect for this, and I advise all my clients to read it. Make sure the entire leadership team knows it inside and out! **John M. Colosimo, Business Owner, and Executive Coach.**

This book is written so that a non-financially-sophisticated business owner can learn how to use financial information to help run a successful business. The breakthrough in this book is that the complex and often bewildering collection of financial ratios that are buried in financial statements are turned into straightforward signals about how the business is doing. Any business owner or manager will benefit from reading this book. **Charles D. Feinstein, Ph.D., CEO, VMN Group LLC.**

At HomeStreet Bank we are always looking for ways to offer value-added services to our business clients, and Duryee has written a book that is ideal for that purpose. His explanation of the technical areas of business finance is easy for the non-financial person to understand, and we believe that his book will assist in our ability to better serve and communicate with our business customers. **David Parr, VP and Regional Manager, HomeStreet Bank.**

I thoroughly enjoyed reading this book and only wish that it had been available to give to my clients when I was a practicing CPA. I think that the chapters on dealing with the CPA and banker are especially valuable and would serve to greatly enhance communications between business owners and their advisors. **Arthur King, CPA, retired.**

60 Minute CFO is an excellent source book for the basics of finance. Duryee has an amazing talent to be succinct. He makes important points in an easy to understand manner and simplifies hard-to-understand concepts. This book is a must read for anyone owning or running a business. **Allen C. Hopson, CPA, CFO.**

Table of Contents

INTRODUCTION

Keep it simple is the over-riding goal of this book. If you are new to business finance you might see its totality as somewhat overwhelming, but it is not if you take it one step at a time. This book explains business finance in words that anyone with a non-financial background can understand. If there is one sentence or paragraph in this book that you do not completely understand, please email me, and I will attempt to explain it better.

Most important, don't try to understand all of this book at one time. Please take it one step at a time. Use the software tools available to you on 60minutecfo.com to help you keep track of your financial condition every month. Give finance 60 minutes a month, a tiny fraction of the time available, and I promise you will quickly understand enough finance to run a successful business. Inch by inch, anything is a cinch!

The Journalist and commentator H.L. Mencken said that "for every complex problem, there is an answer that is clear, simple and wrong." That may be true, but business finance, taken one step at a time, is *not* a complex problem.

THE NEED FOR A COMMON LANGUAGE

What is needed is a common language that allows the business owner, banker, and CPA to communicate.

Business owners believe that if revenue and profit are healthy and growing, banks should be eager to provide the funds necessary to support their company's financial needs.

Bankers are concerned that business owners may not understand the difference between profit and cash flow and may overly rely on debt to support growth.

CPAs provide valuable information in the form of financial statements but often find it challenging to explain how to interpret them. They are described as "those that know the most about what is happening in a business but are the least able to do anything about it." This situation can quickly be resolved with a better understanding of what they can contribute.

This book, written by a former banker, small business owner, and principal in a CPA firm, bridges the communication gap between financial and non-financial executives. It provides a common language that all of these parties can use to help the business achieve financial success.

HOW TO USE THIS BOOK

Read the first four chapters and pause. It will take you no more than 60 minutes, *and you will know all you need to know about analyzing financial statements.* You will learn and understand the key business indicators that your banker and CPA use to evaluate your financial condition, and you will learn how to distinguish between cash flow versus profit.

Then download **Business Mastery** software from 60minutecfo.com and input your financial data every month. When you do that, refer back to the first four chapters to reinforce what the ratios are telling you about your financial strengths and areas that might need improvement. With repetition, the meaning of this data will become second nature to you. Also, be sure to involve your leadership team in this process to explain what you are trying to accomplish and how they can help you. Give it sixty minutes a month. Less than one percent of your time is all that is necessary!

In today's rapidly changing business environment, the business owner, banker, and CPA must understand each other and be on the same page. This book makes it happen. A Business degree is not required. All it takes is 60 minutes a month. Business finance, taken one step at a time, is something that everyone can understand, regardless of their education or background.

THREE STEPS TO UNDERSTANDING BUSINESS FINANCE

1. Look at a few *relationships* on your financial statements in addition to the *numbers*.
2. Understand the difference between *cash flow* and *profit*.
3. Forecast the financial relationships and cash flow to ensure you are moving in the right direction.

This book describes these three steps in simple terms, and the good news is several Excel-based workbooks accompany this book that will do all the calculations for you automatically. Download them at no charge from www.60minutecfo.com.

STEP ONE: UNDERSTANDING FINANCIAL RELATIONSHIPS

The relationships you need to look at are described in chapters one through three. Enter three prior years and then your monthly financial statements in the *Business Mastery* workbook and re-read those chapters every month to refresh your understanding of what those relationships measure. It will not be long before they are second nature to you. Sixty minutes a month is all it takes.

STEP TWO: UNDERSTANDING CASH FLOW

You pay your bills, your debts, and your employees with *cash*, not profit. Understanding cash flow is an essential aspect of business finance, *but not one number on your monthly financial statements pertains to cash flow.*

In 2015 I derived a formula for measuring operating cash flow, and I describe it in chapter four. This description of cash flow allows you to both measure and forecast it utilizing your in-house financial statements. Cash is KING, and the ability to measure it is essential.

STEP THREE: FORECASTING FINANCIAL STATEMENTS

Developing a forecast of your financial statements, cash flow, and financial health for the coming year is the next logical step once you have analyzed the past. Now it is time to venture beyond chapter four. Chapters seven through ten lead you step by step through the forecasting process.

Maybe two percent of business owners do any financial forecasting. After learning how to do it and using *Business Mastery* to do the calculations, you will join this elite group. It is more than worth the effort because lack of planning is one of the biggest single reasons for business failure.

TAKE IT TO THE BANK

Chapter thirteen brings this all together with tips on how to get what you ask for at the bank. The information about your company's financial history and future will include comparisons to the ratio averages for your industry (also available on the 60minuteCFO website).

It is virtually certain that no customer *in the history of the bank* has ever done this. In sixteen years as a banker, it never happened to me once. Your banker will be impressed, and they will likely provide your business the needed financial support. You will get what you ask for at the bank because you will not ask for something you cannot repay.

COMMUNICATE WITH YOUR CPA

Your CPA knows the most about your business's financial condition and has the least ability to do anything about it. This situation needs to change. Your CPA can be an essential member of your advisory team. Read chapter fourteen to discover how to maximize the benefit of this advisory relationship. This book describes the terms of GAAP (Generally Accepted Accounting Principles), which is your CPA's language.

ANALYSIS AND FORECASTING WORKBOOK

Business Mastery calculates cash flow and all the relationships automatically once you input your annual and monthly financial information. Ask your bookkeeper or controller to input your financial information, which is a cinch after customizing the workbook to match your financial statements.

Go over this information each month with your leadership team, who will then be in an excellent position to help you succeed. It is powerful when all your company's key leaders are pulling in the same direction, operating efficiently as a team, and knowing what success looks like. Running a successful business is never the result of one person; it is a team effort.

There are four useful workbooks available with this book. See Appendix I for a description of the complimentary Excel-based workbooks available to download at www.60minutecfo.com.

THE PHASES OF A BUSINESS

Sound financial management of your business remains constant, but your economic and financial condition will change over time. It is worth a few moments to review the following four phases of a business:

1. Start-up
2. High growth
3. Maturity
4. Decline

The revenue growth curve of these phases is as follows:

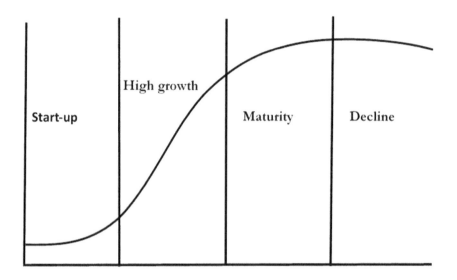

Identifying the phase you are in will give you a frame of reference as you apply the principles outlined in this book to your business.

PHASE 1: START-UP

Entrepreneurs who start businesses have a vision and are highly motivated to make it a reality. They do not, however, usually have much money or experience in running a business. This initial phase of the business has the following characteristics:

1. Lack of capital (equity)
2. Poor, or nonexistent, positive cash flow
3. Inexperienced management

4. Poor or nonexistent financial information

Start-up is a difficult phase. Stress is high, survival is always in question, and work expands well beyond an 8-hour day. We call this the "wonder" phase of business because most of the time, you wonder if you'll survive, and the rest of the time, you wonder why in the world you ever started the business in the first place. If you had known how hard and stressful it would be, you might not have attempted it.

Financial analysis and planning are critical in the wonder phase but are rarely done, primarily due to deficiencies three and four above. Forecasts for the first couple of years can help determine how much capital will ultimately be needed. If that amount is more than can be raised by hitting up relatives, mortgaging the house, and maxing out your credit cards, it would be wise to postpone the start-up.

A realistic forecast of cash flow is also essential. At best, borrowing from a bank in the start-up phase is difficult; it is basically impossible without projections.

Chapters seven through ten on planning are critical in the wonder phase, and chapter eleven explains how to calculate break-even revenue. Armed with break-even information, you can calculate how much you might lose before the business begins to generate a profit, and therefore, how much initial investment will be needed.

Business Mastery, an Excel-based workbook, is available to forecast financial statements, *Business Break-even* is available to calculate break-even and *Business Equipment* is available to determine the advisability of purchasing a vehicle or operating equipment. Download them from the 60 Minute CFO website, www.60minutecfo.com.

PHASE 2: HIGH GROWTH

Hard work, luck, and determination are often enough to get most businesses through the turmoil of the start-up phase and into the high-growth phase. Now things begin to get exciting. Revenue and profits begin to grow rapidly, and this phase has the following characteristics:

1. High growth in revenue and profit
2. Highly strained capital that may be insufficient to sustain the growth
3. Negative operating cash flow
4. Transition management requirements (from seat-of-the-pants to more formal)
5. Better and more complete financial information

While revenue and profit grow at a rapid rate, cash flow is usually not good at all. Chapters four and five explain why this is the case. Negative operating cash flow causes debt to grow to purchase the increased assets that are needed. Additional borrowing is ultimately declined, ironically at a time when the business is doing very well.

The owner is gaining much-needed experience on how to run a business but often has a hard time transitioning from seat-of-the-pants (SOP) style management to the more professional, structured approach that a rapidly growing business requires. Starting a business is fun and exciting but managing a business day-to-day is a lot harder.

Wrong things are done at the wrong time for the wrong reasons. This phase is called the "blunder" phase of business. It is in this phase that many companies fail. They collapse due to the combination of negative cash flow, excessive reliance on debt, and poor management.

That's the bad news. The good news is that you can avoid the problems you encounter in the blunder phase by applying the financial and management principles outlined in this book. They will help you successfully navigate the blunder phase and allow you to join the 15 to 20 percent of businesses that make it to the next phase of business. So keep reading; the solutions are here!

PHASE 3: MATURITY

Maturity is the phase of business that you envisioned when you started. The growth rate has slowed to a manageable pace, and now cash flow is nicely positive. You pay down debt and begin to enjoy the fruits of your sacrifice and hard work of the previous two phases. You join a prestigious country club, go to lovely places on vacation, trade-in the Chevy for a BMW, and pay yourself an excellent salary. You have arrived!

Typical characteristics of this phase are:
1. Strong capital (equity)
2. Solid profitability
3. Positive cash flow
4. Experienced and deep management
5. Timely and accurate financial information

You have survived when the great majority of start-ups fail, and you feel good about that. You have answers for most of the business world's problems and are happy to share them with others around the bar at the country club, even without being asked. You visit the bank with your hat firmly on your head instead of in your hands. You expect the red-carpet treatment, and you get it because the bank now needs you more than you need the bank. This is the "thunder" phase of business. Well, what the heck? You are successful, and you're entitled to thunder.

If you get to the thunder phase, the challenge is to *stay there*. This book will help you do that, but it is not as easy as it might seem. Growth is now more modest, and complacency and overconfidence become the norm. As owners age, they naturally become more conservative. The thunder phase of business is a great place to be, but it takes careful planning and diligence to *stay* there.

Chris Petersen, a successful Division I football coach, got it right when he said:

> *It's much harder to stay up near the top than to get there. These kids don't know that, but I do.*

If you follow the principles in this book, you will be better equipped and more likely to stay in the thunder phase of business. If I had known everything I know now when I was running my own business, I can tell you that I would have been more successful.

PHASE 4: DECLINE

Like the wonder and blunder phases, the decline phase is difficult. Owners are now well into their sixties, and age has become a partner in the business. The desire to take any significant risks is gone. Conservation of existing assets is the primary goal, and younger managers chafe at the status quo attitude that exists.

This phase of the business has the following characteristics:

1. Strong capital (equity)
2. Strong but declining cash flow
3. Solid but declining growth and profitability
4. Complacent, detached, status quo ownership
5. Adversity to risk

Competition now eats away at the company's market share as more aggressive firms grow at faster rates. Cash flow and net profit are good but declining. This phase of the business is called the "plunder" phase, and the company gradually declines. A business in this phase either continues to decline, or ownership can launch it into another high-growth blunder phase, which may be every bit as challenging as the first one.

Owners in the plunder phase should either sell the business or let the next generation take over, but this can be difficult and painful. No one wants to feel unneeded or outdated. Egos are a problem, but the business's ultimate health and survival depend on new and energetic management.

WHAT IS YOUR PHASE OF BUSINESS?

Think about the business phase that you are in as you read this book and put your financial information in that context. Many of your financial ratios won't look good in the wonder and blunder phases because you aren't well-established, but your goal to achieve financial strength should be constant and unwavering, and you need to know how financial strength looks.

You need to get to the thunder phase and then *stay* there, and with consistent planning and application of the principles outlined in this book, you will!

HIGH BUSINESS FAILURE RATE

Estimates vary, but the consensus is that 80 to 85 percent of all businesses that start fail within the first ten years. There are lots of reasons for this, but the most prevalent are:

1. Lack of planning
2. Poor leadership
3. Lack of financial understanding
4. Negative cash flow
5. Lack of a valuable product or service

Practicing the principles in this book will help you with the first four. Number five is a difficult problem, but it is rarely the cause of failure. The first four are.

BRIDGING THE COMMUNICATION GAP

This book bridges the financial communication gap that exists between business owners and their financial advisors. It explains in plain English the terms, concepts, and fundamentals of business finance so that business owners can communicate with their banker, CPA, bookkeeper, and CFO. All it takes is 60 minutes a month.

UNDERSTANDING FINANCE IS A JOURNEY, NOT A DESTINATION

Learning about business finance is not a destination. You are about to start on a journey. All you have is a canoe and a paddle, but it is a sturdy, well-built canoe. It will survive the fiercest of storms, and you will get stronger as you paddle. You might tire at some point and ask, "Are we there yet?" The answer will always be, "No, not yet."

Take your time. Don't rush this. The reality is that learning about how best to run a business is a *lifetime* journey. Pablo Casals, a reasonably proficient cello player, was asked why he practiced three hours a day at the age of 93. His response was "Because I believe I am making progress." I have been working in business finance in one form or another since 1965, but I learn new things every year. I don't call that discouraging, I call it making progress.

Just when you think you know it all about how to run a business, you will learn something new. It is fun and exciting, and, as a non-financial person, you will be surprised at how easy it will be.

SUMMARY

Business Mastery is an Excel-based workbook that performs all the calculations discussed in this book. It is powerful because important concepts like cash flow and financial health are measured, analyzed, and forecasted.

With this software, you can observe past trends and then establish a forecast for your income statement, balance sheet, cash flow, and financial ratios. *Business Mastery* is designed to assist you in communicating with outside advisors such as your banker and CPA.

Download it from www.60minutecfo.com and use it monthly to track your performance, communicate with your leadership team, and educate your banker.

Remember that learning about business finance is a journey, not a destination. The goal is not to be a financial expert but to know enough to communicate with your banker and CPA. This basic knowledge is your responsibility as the leader of your company. Take it one step at a time and always be thinking about what is new with your business and how that might affect you from a financial standpoint.

Keep this book handy and refer to it from time-to-time to refresh your memory. Repetition is the key, so be sure to input your financial statements every month. You will make progress as well.

The next chapter begins a discussion of the financial analysis process with a focus on the balance sheet.

Keep it simple, and keep on paddling!!

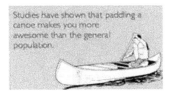

CHAPTER ONE: THE BALANCE SHEET

1

INTRODUCTION

In 1979, a contractor friend of mine came to me and said, "Dave, I have a great opportunity to develop a piece of real estate into luxury condominiums, and I want you to be involved in it." He knew how to build, and I knew finance, so he thought we would make a good team.

He told me that the person who owned the land was willing to contribute his property for a percentage of the profits. My friend obtained one hundred percent financing for construction, and he assured me that all of the twelve units in the six-story building would be *pre-sold* before completion. All we had to do was offer a personal guarantee and put up our homes as collateral.

This came as close to a "no brainer" as I had ever seen. What could possibly go wrong? We stood to make a lot of money without investing a cent! I patiently explained to my wife why this would be a great opportunity ("trust me, honey, this will make us a lot of money"), and she reluctantly agreed.

So, there we were. All debt and no equity, with a construction loan of $5 million. Maybe there was some *potential* risk, but it was a "sure thing." All we had to do was build, sell, and take the profits to the bank.

Unfortunately, it didn't work, and I'll tell you "the rest of the story" at the end of this chapter.

BALANCE SHEET - THE RODNEY DANGERFIELD FINANCIAL STATEMENT

Business owners tend to give their balance sheet only a cursory look. I call it the Rodney Dangerfield of financial statements. It gets no respect because it has no revenue and no profits. It just sits there telling you things that you mostly already knew, like the amount of cash in the bank. The balance sheet does tell you how much equity you have, but this is somewhat of an abstract concept. You can't see it, you can't touch it, and you can't spend it. What good is equity as far as the operation of the business is concerned? It just sits there on the balance sheet.

The balance sheet may lack excitement, but it is the foundation of your business, and a weak balance sheet is where most companies get into financial trouble. Do you want excitement? Let your balance sheet go south, and you'll have plenty. Read on to find out why.

CONTENTS OF THE BALANCE SHEET

The balance sheet is a statement of assets, liabilities, and equity.

Assets are what you **own**, such as accounts receivable (money due from your customers), inventory (items in stock that you sell), and equipment (machinery, vehicles, etc.). Liabilities are what you **owe**, such as accounts payable (bills from vendors) and bank loans, both lines of credit for seasonal needs and long-term loans for purchasing equipment.

Equity is whatever is left after you subtract the liabilities from the assets, as follows:

Assets	*Minus*	**Liabilities**	*Equals*	**Equity**
what you own		what you owe		what's left for owners

Stated another way, the basic formula for the balance sheet is:

Assets	*Equals*	**Liabilities**	*Plus*	**Equity**
total funds invested in the business		funds supplied by creditors		funds supplied by owners

The diagram on the following page illustrates the balance sheet.

Current Assets		Current Liabilities
cash		bank line of credit
accounts receivable		trade payables
inventory		accrued expenses
prepaid expenses		bank debt, current portion
	Working Capital	Long-Term Debt
		bank debt, long-term
Fixed Assets		capital leases
furniture and fixtures		inter-company loans
vehicles and equipment		other long-term debt
Other Assets		Equity
investments		capital
memberships, etc.		retained earnings

Funds in the business   Source of the funds

DEFINITION OF TERMS

Current assets

Current assets are those assets that will turn into cash within twelve months from the date of the balance sheet. Examples include cash, accounts receivable, inventory, and prepaid expenses (expenses that are invoiced but not due).

Fixed assets

Fixed assets include such things as furniture, fixtures, equipment, and leasehold improvements. Fixed assets are listed on your balance sheet at what you paid for them (cost), less the amount that has been written off (accumulated depreciation). Gross fixed assets minus accumulated depreciation equals net fixed assets.

Most equipment is written off in five years or less. A truck that costs $30,000 would be written off at $6,000 per year, assuming zero salvage at the end of the fifth year. This is called "straight-line" depreciation. Your CPA will provide you with a depreciation schedule and advise you on the annual write-off (depreciation) for any fixed asset you purchase.

The current income tax regulations allow you to use various methods for accelerating the depreciation write-off of an asset, and use this accelerated depreciation to reduce income taxes. Always use straight-line depreciation on your internally produced financial statements because accelerated depreciation artificially lowers both the value of your assets and your profit. Only use accelerated depreciation for your tax return.

Other assets

Other assets are those that are not directly involved in the operation of your business. These include cash value of life insurance, club memberships, investments, and intangible assets. Intangible assets, such as a copyright or trademark, are routinely subtracted from your assets and equity by the bank in analyzing your balance sheet since they probably have little or no value as collateral for a loan from the bank. A country club membership also might fall into this category. Do not be surprised if the bank deducts the value of your intangible assets from both your total assets and equity.

Current liabilities

Current liabilities are those obligations that you owe others that are due within twelve months from the date of the balance sheet. They include accounts payable, bank line of credit, accrued expenses (those that are due but not invoiced), and the current portion of long-term bank debt (the total of the next twelve principle payments due on your long-term debt).

Long-term liabilities

Long-term liabilities are those loans that are due twelve months or more from the date of the balance sheet and include a long-term bank loan or some leases payable on equipment. These obligations are listed net of the current portion of long-term debt that is included in current liabilities.

Equity

Equity is the amount invested in the business by owners. It is also referred to as net worth, capital, or net book value. It consists of the initial funds invested in the business plus earnings retained in the business (not paid out to owners) since the inception of the company.

BALANCE SHEET RELATIONSHIPS

Looking at the *numbers* will never reveal the financial strength of your balance sheet. You could have a net worth of $10 million or have $1 million in the bank and still have a weak balance sheet. Relationships (ratios or key business indicators) determine the financial condition of your balance sheet, and we will discuss those that are routinely used by bankers and other analysts for that purpose.

We want to learn two things from the balance sheet; the liquidity and safety of your business.

LIQUIDITY

I define liquidity as *the ability to pay bills*. Since current assets are those assets that will *turn to cash* within one year, and current liabilities are those obligations that are *due* within one year, it makes sense to compare one to the other to determine your ability to pay your bills.

Liquidity is calculated as follows:

Current assets
Current liabilities   =   **Current ratio**

This relationship, called the current ratio, is a measure of liquidity, the ability to pay bills.

To interpret this ratio, imagine a dollar sign on it. A current ratio of 1.53 means that you have $1.53 of current assets (those assets that will turn to cash in 12 months) to pay every $1.00 of current liabilities (those obligations that are due within 12 months). The higher the current ratio, the more liquid you are, and the abler you are to pay your debts when they are due.

Firms with low liquidity get into serious trouble quickly in the event of a sudden downturn in the economy. Creditors expect to be paid, and they are quick to take legal action if necessary. Firms that had low liquidity were the ones that quickly got into trouble during the great recession of 2008.

Liquidity and working capital

Working capital is the difference between current assets and current liabilities.

	Current assets	those that turn into cash in 12 months
Minus	Current liabilities	those that are due in 12 months
Equals	Working capital	

Obviously, you need at least as much in current assets as you have in current liabilities, or you will not be able to pay them, but the fact is that you need *more* current assets than current liabilities. This is true because you will not pay very many bills with some of your current assets, like inventory and prepaid expenses.

An adequate current ratio is 1.50, which means that you have 1.5 times more in current assets than current liabilities.

An excellent current ratio is 2.00, which means that you have 2.0 times more in current assets than current liabilities.

In my experience working with small businesses, there is a perfect correlation between successful firms and those firms that have a current ratio of around 2.00. Successful firms have strong working capital, and they do not have problems paying their bills when due, even during an economic downturn. Liquidity and adequate working capital are where you live every day. You need to be able to pay your bills, or you will have serious difficulty.

If you have $100,000 in current liabilities and you want a current ratio of 2.00, then you need to have at least $200,000 in current assets, or $100,000 in working capital, as follows:

$200,000	Current assets
($100,000)	Current liabilities
$100,000	Working capital

To put that another way, if you have $200,000 in current assets, the most you can have is $100,000 in current liabilities.

A good range for the current ratio is 1.50 to 2.00 for most businesses. That means you have between $1.50 and $2.00 of current assets to pay every $1.00 of current liabilities.

Fixing low liquidity

If your current ratio is below 1.50, you need to work on getting it to at least that level. The second rule of business finance is to remember the first rule – keep it simple. Suppose you have current assets of $150,000 and current liabilities of $110,000, a 1.36 current ratio. You need to reduce current liabilities to $100,000 to have a current ratio of at least 1.50. This is very simple to calculate as follows:

$$\frac{\$150,000}{1.5} \quad = \quad \$100,000$$

You need to generate $10,000 from operations, which means at least $10,000 of operating cash flow (see chapter four). You can do this by any one or more of the following actions:

1. Increase your net profit margin (see chapter two)
2. Reduce your receivable days (see chapter three)
3. Reduce your inventory days (see chapter three)
4. Loan the company $10,000 on a long-term loan

Generating an additional $10,000 in operating cash flow to reduce current liabilities may or not be easy, but it is simple to calculate. In the above example, your goal is to have $50,000 in working capital, which is the minimum required for satisfactory liquidity.

Excess liquidity
The higher the current ratio, the higher the liquidity, so the question often arises about whether a current ratio of 2.50 or 3.00 is better than a current ratio of 2.00. The answer is no, it is not "better," but it is more "liquid."

A very high current ratio is going to mean having a significant amount of money in the bank. This is not exactly "bad," but it is also not a very good use of the company's resources since cash earns very little if any return. It might be better to distribute out excess cash to the owner and then loan it back to the company if necessary. Very high liquidity is often one of a firm's characteristics in the plunder phase of business.

SAFETY

I define safety as *the ability to withstand adversity*. Adversity may be anything from a downturn in the economy to a natural disaster of some sort.

Safety is measured by comparing total liabilities (funds provided by creditors) to equity (funds provided by owners). The higher this ratio, the less safe or more risky the business. The firms that have the heaviest debt in relation to their equity at the time of adversity are the ones that are the least safe and the least likely to survive. This is common sense since creditors get upset when they are not paid in the event of a recession and eventually take legal action.

Safety is measured by the debt-to-equity ratio, as follows:

$$\frac{\textbf{Total liabilities}}{\textbf{Equity}} \quad = \quad \textbf{Debt-to-equity ratio}$$

To visualize this ratio, put a dollar sign on it. A debt-to-equity ratio of 2.15 means that you have $2.15 in liabilities for every $1.00 of equity. In other words, the creditors have over twice as much invested in the business as the owner. The higher the ratio, the less safe you are.

The debt-to-equity ratio (also referred to as the debt-to-worth or debt-to-net-worth ratio) is one of your banker's favorite ratios because the bank is concerned about the riskiness of your business. If this ratio gets too high, you will have increased risk and be a much less desirable loan prospect.

A debt-to-equity ratio of 3.00 or higher means that the creditors have three times more invested in the business than the owner, and for most industries, this will raise red flags at the bank. You will be put on their watchlist and not supplied with additional loans until you reduce to 2.00 or below.

How much risk is too much?

Determining the optimal risk level for your business depends on several factors:

1. **Your risk tolerance.**
    Risk tolerance is different for every individual and will change as your situation changes (age, family, financial responsibilities, etc.). When you are young, you may be willing to take on more risk than when you are over sixty and want to ensure that you have security for your retirement.

2. **The status of the economy.**
    If a downturn or recession is forecast, it would be wise to reduce debt and make your balance sheet stronger during tough times. Conversely, if a strong economy is forecasted, it may be a good time to aggressively expand your business

and take on more debt in the process. Risk will be higher but probably tolerable if no recession is forecasted.

3. **The status of the industry.**

   If a downturn in your industry is forecasted, it would not be a good time to take on a big expansion project and use debt to fund it. On the other hand, if your debt-to-equity ratio is low at the time of a downturn, it could be an advantageous time to acquire other businesses at a depressed price or grow your business and take on additional debt in the process.

4. **The age of the owner.**

   As a rule, business owners over sixty-five are less interested in taking on more risk. They are planning for retirement and understandably want to ensure that their retirement funds survive as long as they do. This may not be a good time for taking big risks with the family retirement nest egg.

Understanding the concept of safety and risk is essential for every business owner, and you should regularly monitor the safety of your business. This monitoring ensures that you will operate within your risk tolerance and in a fashion consistent with the economy and the industry's condition. It also helps to ensure that you will avoid added scrutiny at the bank.

A good range for the debt-to-equity ratio is 1.00 to 1.50 for most businesses. That is between $1.00 and $1.50 of debt for every $1.00 of equity.

Safety in a 100-year event

When I wrote this book in 2017, it was impossible to contemplate what happened in 2020. The pandemic caused revenue to virtually disappear for companies in some industries like travel and hospitality. Without substantial help from the government, most of them would have gone out of business, especially those with a high debt-to-equity ratio. The range for the debt-to-equity-ratio outlined above is appropriate for "normal" times but is far too high for a 100-year event.

I don't have a good answer for how to plan for such an occurrence, except to say that it now has to be in our collective consciousness. We can only hope that something like COVID 19 truly is a 100-year event, but it behooves all of us to remember that it *can* happen and adjust our thought accordingly. Thanks to climate change, we are now having "50-year storms" much more frequently, and rapid technological change can make some industries obsolete.

These are challenging times to be in business, and the result of all this is perhaps to lower our sights as to what might be an acceptable debt-to-equity range. I leave it to you to reflect on this and come to the conclusions that seem appropriate to your particular situation. I have had forty years to observe what I feel is a good safety range, but the next forty years probably will not mirror that experience, so I urge you to give this careful thought.

A range of 0.50 to 1.00 is much more conservative and worthy of consideration.

Fixing high risk

A high debt-to-equity ratio indicates a lack of capital, which is one of the characteristics of firms in the start-up and blunder phase of business. The solution is not complicated. You need to make sure that you have positive operating cash flow (see chapter four), particularly in the high growth phase (see chapter six), so that you can build equity. No one can grow as fast as they want, so you need to manage growth carefully.

It is also essential to have a high net profit margin (see chapter two). A combination of managed growth, keeping earnings in the business, and high profitability will quickly result in a lowering of your debt-to-equity ratio.

Keep it simple, focus on four things:
1. Managed growth
2. Positive operating cash flow
3. High-profit margins
4. Retaining earnings in the business

You will be surprised how quickly these four actions result in lowering your risk to an acceptable level. Then make sure you keep it there going forward.

BALANCE SHEET ADJUSTMENTS

You cannot change your financial statements, but it may be appropriate to alter some of the account balances when calculating these ratios.

FIXED ASSET ADJUSTMENTS

Fixed assets are listed on your balance sheet at the purchase cost, less accumulated depreciation. Your fixed assets may be understated based upon their actual market values, especially in the case of land and buildings. If your fixed assets are undervalued, it is okay for financial analysis purposes to adjust your assets' value to their approximate fair market value, add the increase in value to your equity, and then re-calculate the debt-to-equity ratio.

Use caution in doing this since actual market values are sometimes difficult to determine with precision. Still, this upward adjustment will have the impact of lowering your debt-to-equity ratio and, therefore, your risk. This adjustment is particularly applicable if the business owns real estate that has appreciated in value. If you make this adjustment, explain to your banker your assumptions and how you arrived at the increased values.

This adjustment is solely for purposes of calculating the debt-to-equity ratio since your financial statements are prepared according to generally accepted accounting principles (GAAP) and cannot be altered.

INTANGIBLE ASSET ADJUSTMENTS

Intangible assets, such as a copyright or trademark, will be subtracted from your total assets and equity by the banker since these types of assets produce little or no value to the bank as collateral for a loan.. This adjustment will lower your equity and therefore increase your debt-to-equity ratio.

SHAREHOLDER LOANS

Loans payable to shareholders represent money that the owners have loaned to the company, usually on a temporary basis. If these loans are subordinated to bank debt (they cannot be paid back without prior bank approval), the bank considers the loans to be the same as equity, subtracts them from your liabilities, and adds them to equity. This adjustment will result in a lower debt-to-equity ratio, increased safety, and increased borrowing capacity. It is in your best interest to subordinate shareholder debt to the bank debt for this reason.

TREND ANALYSIS

Look at the trends over three to four years because reviewing your balance sheet for just one period may be misleading. Your business may currently have low liquidity but improving each year. Or you may have good but deteriorating safety. Examining these ratios' trends over three to four years is an integral part of the analysis process.

INDUSTRY COMPARISONS

Whenever possible, you should look at ratio averages for businesses in your industry. The publication that contains this data is *Annual Statement Studies*, published by Risk Management Association (RMA). Check with your local library, ask your banker or CPA, or go to www.60minutecfo.com and ask for this information, which I will supply at no cost.

Input your industry's ratio averages in **Business Mastery** and discuss how you compare to them in your business's analysis narrative. You will be held in very high esteem by your banker since virtually no other bank customer has ever done this. I was a banker for sixteen years and never had one client include RMA averages in their analysis.

INTERNAL STANDARDS

Industry averages are helpful, but your company standards are the most meaningful for your business. Determine how liquid or safe you want to be, and then manage your business according to those standards.

CASH VERSUS ACCRUAL ACCOUNTING

Cash-basis accounting records revenue when cash is *received* for goods or services and records expenses when cash is *paid out*. Accrual-basis accounting records revenue when it is *earned* whether or not cash has been received, and an expense when it is *incurred* whether or not cash has been paid out.

Suppose expenses are paid in advance in accrual-basis accounting, like a six-month insurance premium. In that case, a *prepaid expense* account is established and listed as an asset on the balance sheet. One-sixth of the amount is recognized as an expense in the first month, and the prepaid expense account is then amortized (expensed) in the next five months. Under cash-basis accounting, the entire six-month payment would be considered an expense at the time of payment.

A business may be on a cash-basis accounting for income tax purposes (check with your CPA to see if you qualify for this), but always prepare financial statements on an accrual-basis accounting. Accounts receivable, prepaid expenses, accrued liabilities, and accounts payable are not listed on a cash-basis balance sheet, even though they exist.

Therefore, it is impossible to get an accurate picture of your financial condition if some assets and liabilities are not listed.

A cash-basis financial statement makes it impossible to analyze either your income statement or your balance sheet properly. The case study uses accrual-basis accounting throughout this book, and it is what your internal bookkeeping system should reflect for financial statement purposes. Make sure your accounting department or bookkeeper does not publish cash-basis financial statements.

ACCELERATED DEPRECIATION

Accelerated depreciation may be used for your tax return but should *not* be used for your internally prepared income statement because it distorts actual profitability for the period. Always use straight-line depreciation for your income statement and balance sheet.

CASE STUDY: DURSON DISTRIBUTORS

Durson Distributors is a wholesale distributor of electrical supplies located in North Carolina. The owner and founder is Julian Durson, age sixty-nine, and his son, Allen, age forty, is the sales manager. Julian's wife, Sara, is not involved in the business. Julian founded the company thirty-five years ago using personal savings and a second mortgage on his home. Durson Distributors is the case study used throughout this book for illustrative purposes. The next page illustrates the balance sheets for Durson Distributors over the last three years.

Balance sheet (000)

	20X1	20X2	20X3
Cash	$154	$202	$318
Accounts receivable	601	595	510
Inventory	463	445	497
Other current assets	37	39	41
Total Current Assets	$1,255	$1,281	$1,366
Gross fixed assets	862	887	895
Accumulated depreciation	(602)	(652)	(700)
Net fixed assets	260	235	195
Other assets	35	37	32
Total Assets	$1,550	$1,553	$1,593
Line of credit-bank	-0-	-0-	-0-
Trade accounts payable	451	359	300
Accrued expenses	38	21	20
Current portion long-term bank debt	39	52	31
Total Current Liabilities	$528	$432	$351
Long-term bank debt	147	76	67
Shareholder debt	-0-	-0-	-0-
Total Liabilities	$675	$508	$418
Equity	$875	$1,045	$1,175
Total Liabilities and Equity	$1,550	$1,553	$1,593

BALANCE SHEET ANALYSIS

LIQUIDITY

The following are the current ratios for Durson:

	20X1	20X2	20X3	Industry Average[1]
Current Ratio	2.38	2.97	3.89	1.60

[1] Industry averages for Durson Distributors throughout this book are taken from Risk Management Associates *Annual Statement Studies* NAICS 423610. Ask your banker or CPA for a copy of these ratios for your industry. They are also available at no charge by requesting them at www.60minutecfo.com.

The current ratio of 3.89 in 20X3 means that the company has $3.89 of current assets to pay every $1.00 of current liabilities. The trend is up since 20X1, and it is much higher than the industry average of 1.60.

You can easily see by looking at this ratio that this company's liquidity is excellent in 20X3 and is trending upward.

1.50 to 2.00 is a good standard for most industries.

SAFETY

The following are the debt-to-equity ratios for Durson:

	20X1	20X2	20X3	Industry Average
Debt-to-Equity Ratio	0.77	0.49	0.36	1.70

The debt-to-equity ratio of 0.36 in 20X3 means that the company has $.36 in debt for every $1.00 of equity. This ratio has been trending downward since 20X1 and is quite a bit lower than the industry average of 1.70. At the end of 20X3, Mr. Durson has roughly three times more invested in the business than the creditors. The lower the ratio, the higher the safety and lower the risk. A debt-to-equity ratio of 0.36 is a safe position, and it is getting safer.

1.00 to 1.50 is a good standard for most industries.

DURSON BALANCE SHEET SUMMARY

We conclude that the balance sheet for Durson in 20X3 has excellent liquidity and safety. The trends are good, and the company compares very favorably to industry averages.

This analysis was simple and easy to do. Just two relationships indicated the balance sheet's strength, and the good news is that Business Mastery does these calculations for you. Keep it simple.

SUMMARY

The balance sheet is the foundation of your business, and it needs to be strong for you to build a successful business. Two things will determine balance sheet strength—liquidity, the ability to pay bills, and safety, the ability to withstand adversity. The current ratio measures liquidity, and the debt-to-equity ratio measures safety. Not twenty things. Not ten things. *Just two.*

A current ratio of 3.89 means that you have $3.89 in current assets to pay every dollar of current liabilities. That means that you have working capital of $2.89 ($3.89 minus $1.00). The higher this ratio, the more liquid you are.

Liquidity is necessary because it is where you operate financially every day. You need to be able to pay your bills and other obligations on a timely basis. Firms get into trouble quickly if there is insufficient liquidity, and it is why some of your customers don't pay you promptly. They lack sufficient liquidity and working capital, and they solve this problem by not paying some of their accounts payable when they are due.

There is a virtual 100% correlation between successful firms and good working capital. Calculate this ratio monthly and manage your business to be sufficiently liquid, with strong working capital. *Working capital* is the difference between current assets and current liabilities.

A debt-to-equity ratio of 0.36 means that you have $.36 in debt for every $1.00 of equity. You should manage your safety to avoid being caught in a recession with a high debt-to-equity ratio and high risk. You want to be healthy and safe in the face of adversity.

The trend over several years is essential in analyzing these ratios and comparing your business to industry averages (RMA) if they are available. A percentage analysis also helps determine the trend of your assets, liabilities, and equity as a percentage of total assets, and *Business Mastery* calculates this for you.

Recalculate ratios using values for assets that have been adjusted to their fair market value versus their value on your balance sheet (book value) if you have reason to believe there is a significant disparity. You cannot change your balance sheet, which is prepared using generally accepted accounting principles (GAAP), but you can make these adjustments for purposes of this ratio analysis. This adjustment will yield different results for your ratios, particularly if you have real estate in your business that has appreciated. Intangible assets, if any, should be subtracted from total assets and equity for purposes of your analysis.

This analysis of the balance sheet is neither complicated nor time-consuming. Two ratios, measuring liquidity and safety, are sufficient to indicate your balance sheet's strength, and looking at three or four years reveals any significant trends.

Do not worry about the formulas in this chapter. *Business Mastery*, an Excel-based workbook, is available that will calculate these ratios for you automatically. Download it from www.60minutecfo.com.

THE REST OF THE STORY

Oh, and now let me share the rest of the ill-fated condo story. We completed construction of the building in 1981, just in time for the prime rate to peak out at over 20 percent, before or since the first and only time in the history of business in America happened.

This high prime rate was an unexpected and unique occurrence, and we were distressed to discover that no one was willing to buy a luxury condominium when the prime rate was over 20 percent. It was my "100-year event." The bank foreclosed on their $6 million loan and came after my partner and me, who had guaranteed the loan. After 18 months of legal wrangling, I wound up settling my obligations for a manageable amount. Not a paltry sum, but enough to permanently emblazon this principle in my mind.

It was a stressful time, and I was reminded of what I already knew, that the balance sheet is the foundation of the business. It was enticing not to invest any money upfront, but all debt and no equity is very risky. A "sure thing" quickly evaporated when adversity struck, and we were not able to survive. An important lesson, re-learned!

The next chapter will discuss analyzing the income statement.
Keep it simple and keep on paddling!

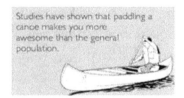
Studies have shown that paddling a canoe makes you more awesome than the general population.

CHAPTER TWO: THE INCOME STATEMENT

2

INTRODUCTION

There is no Rodney Dangerfield effect with the income statement. It gets lots of respect, but business owners typically do not get the information about profitability that they urgently need. This chapter will describe how to look at your income statement to measure profitability correctly.

Most, if not all, business owners look only at the numbers on their income statement. "What was my revenue?" "What was my net profit?" It is not incorrect to do this, but it is not sufficient and may even be misleading. Just like the balance sheet, you need to look at some key *relationships* in addition to the numbers to adequately measure profitability.

The business that I co-owned and operated was a service business, and it was successful from the outset. We made money and had good cash flow. I'll share with you what we did to measure our profitability at the end of this chapter. Keep reading to learn "the rest of the story."

CONTENTS OF THE INCOME STATEMENT

The income statement is a statement of revenue, expenses, and net profit. It is a *period* statement since it covers a specified period like a month, quarter, year, etc. The income statement differs from the balance sheet, which is a position statement for one day only.

The diagram on the following page illustrates the format of the income statement. This document is also referred to as the Profit and Loss statement, or the "P&L."

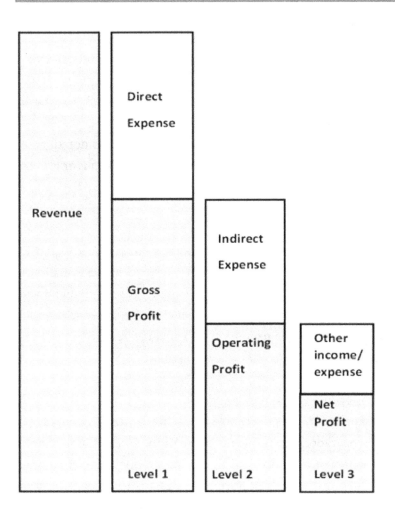

THREE LEVELS OF PROFITABILITY

As you can see from this diagram, there are not one but *three* levels of profitability: gross profit, operating profit, and net profit.

Expenses are separated into:
1. **direct,** those that directly contribute to producing revenue
2. **indirect,** those that are not directly related to producing revenue (also referred to as general and administrative, G&A, overhead, or operating expenses), and
3. **other,** those income and expense items that are not directly related to the operation of the business, such as a gain or loss on the sale of a vehicle.

Direct expenses include direct wages, shipping, lease or rental of operations equipment, and the cost of goods sold. Indirect expenses include advertising, office, travel and entertainment, professional fees, insurance, and administrative wages. Some expenses are both direct and indirect. Examples would be payroll tax, which is on direct wages and administrative wages. Other examples may include rent, depreciation, and insurance.

If an expense is both direct and indirect, you need to decide if it is worth the effort to separate it. This decision hinges on two things; how easy it is to make the separation and the significance of the amount. If it is more trouble than it is worth to do this, I recommend including the entire amount in indirect expense. The important thing is to be consistent in this treatment so that you have comparability from one period to the next.

LEVEL ONE – GROSS PROFIT
Revenue minus direct expense equals gross profit. This is the first and most important level of profitability.

Many companies, especially service companies, do not reflect direct expenses on their income statement in the mistaken belief that they do not have direct expenses. Failure to identify direct expenses is a serious mistake because the gross profit is the primary driver of profitability. If this applies to your firm, make a point to sit down with your bookkeeper and carefully determine your direct expenses and gross profit.

The gross profit is what I call "the front line" in the war of profitability. If you lose the battle at this level, you are going to lose the war. By studying the diagram, you can see that it is the gross profit, not revenue, that pays indirect expenses and generates an operating profit. Therefore, it behooves you to focus your immediate attention on your gross profit.

LEVEL TWO – OPERATING PROFIT
Gross profit minus indirect expense equals operating profit. You can still lose the profitability war at this level if your indirect expenses are too high. If this profitability level is low, it is either due to a poor gross profit margin, high indirect expenses, or both.

If you lose the battle here, the war is lost, and without first examining the gross profit, you will not know what corrective action you need to take. Analyzing how to increase your gross profit is a very different exercise than determining how to reduce indirect expenses, and you need to know where to place your efforts.

LEVEL THREE – NET PROFIT
Operating profit plus other income, minus other expense, and minus interest expense equals net profit. Other income includes such things as interest income or a gain on the sale of an asset. Other expense includes

a loss on the sale of an asset, or some other non-operating expense. Interest expense on interest-bearing debt is the final account included in this "other" category.

THREE PROFITABILITY RATIOS

You need to look at *key relationships* in addition to the *numbers* to measure profitability. $1 million in net profit may sound good, but not if you have $2 billion in revenue. That would be virtually a break-even year and a disaster. It is important to know what you have in net profit *in relationship to something else.*

LEVEL ONE: GROSS PROFIT MARGIN (GPM)

Revenue minus direct expense is equal to the Gross Profit. When expressed as a percent of revenue, it is the gross profit margin.

$$\frac{\text{Gross profit}}{\text{Revenue}} \quad = \quad \text{Gross profit margin (GPM)}$$

The gross profit margin is the most important ratio that you calculate. It is the first level of profitability and what I call the front line of attack in winning the war for profitability in your business. It is tough to make it up below this level if you lose the battle here. You need to know your gross profit margin and if it is trending up or down. The problem is that most CEOs go right past the gross profit margin and look at the bottom line. How much did I make in profit? is the primary question.

Your gross profit margin is critical because a small decline of 1.0% will significantly impact your net profit. If your revenue is $5,000,000, as an example, a decline of 1.0% in the gross profit margin is equal to $50,000 in lost gross profit. If your net profit margin is 5.0%, a drop of 1.0% is 20% of your net profit, as follows:

	$	%	$	%
Revenue	5,000,000	100.0	5,000,000	100.0
Direct exp	3,100,000	62.0	3,150,000	63.0
Gross Profit	**1,900,000**	**38.0**	**1,850,000**	**37.0**
Indirect exp	1,600,000	32.0	1,600,000	32.0
Operating profit	**300,000**	**6.0**	**250,000**	**5.0**
Other exp	(50,000)	(1.0)	(50,000	(1.0)
Net profit	**250,000**	**5.0**	**200,000**	**4.0**

A loss of 1.0% in the gross profit margin has caused a decline of 20% in the net profit margin. Management needs to determine why this happened and how to correct it.

Most service firms do not show a gross profit on their income statement because direct expenses are sometimes referred to as "cost of goods sold." Since a service firm does not sell a product and therefore does not have cost of goods sold, many have an income statement that looks like this:

> Revenue
> (Minus expenses)
> Operating profit

If this is the case with your firm, the solution is to re-format your income statement, listing direct and indirect expenses, and begin measuring your gross profit margin. You will then be able to determine what it *should be* over several periods of observation. This information will allow you to determine the costs of providing your services and set your prices on an informed basis, thereby increasing your profitability.

Scrutinize your expenses to determine which ones are caused by and directly related to revenue, and then be consistent so that you have comparability from one period to the next. Use your best judgment, and then go forward on that basis.

All companies have a gross profit, and it is the most important ratio that you will calculate. Unfortunately, it is the Rodney Dangerfield of ratios. In over 40 years of discussing profit margins, I have never had a CEO tell me what the gross profit margin is or *should be* in their business, not one. Watch your gross profit margin like a hawk, and when it declines even 0.1 percent, make sure you find out why and take corrective action, if possible. A minimal decline in your gross profit margin causes a much more significant reduction in your operating and net profit margin!

It behooves you to know your gross profit margin and, more important, determine what it *should* be. Lean on your CPA, bookkeeper, or CFO to assist you in correctly formatting your income statement with both direct and indirect expenses.

There is no universal standard for the gross profit margin. It will vary depending on your industry, your product mix, how efficiently you operate, and how intelligently you price your products.

What is universal is that if you want to maximize profitability in your business, you must pay close attention to your gross profit, both in dollars and as a percent of revenue.

LEVEL TWO: OPERATING PROFIT MARGIN (OPM)

Gross profit minus indirect expense is equal to the operating profit. When expressed as a percent of revenue, it is the operating profit margin.

$$\frac{\text{Operating profit}}{\text{Revenue}} = \text{Operating profit margin (OPM)}$$

A low operating profit results from either a low gross profit or excess indirect expenses, or both. By measuring your gross profit margin and your operating profit margin, you can determine whether to increase prices, reduce indirect expenses, or both.

LEVEL THREE: NET PROFIT MARGIN (NPM)

Operating profit plus or minus other income and expense is equal to the net profit. When expressed as a percent of revenue, it is the net profit margin.

$$\frac{\text{Net profit}}{\text{Revenue}} = \text{Net profit margin (NPM)}$$

Always calculate the net profit margin on a pre-tax basis to be comparable to all other forms of business regardless of how they are treated for tax purposes.

When analyzed in concert, the gross profit margin, operating profit margin, and net profit margin are useful in determining if you have any profitability issues.

Example:

Revenue	$4,805	100.0%	
(Direct expenses)	(3,118)	(64.9%)	
Gross Profit	1,687	35.1%	**GPM level one**
(Indirect expenses)	(1,521)	31.7%	
Operating Profit	166	3.4%	**OPM level two**
Other income/expense	(19)	0.4%	
Net Profit	$147	3.0%	**NPM level three**

The three profit levels should be expressed as a dollar amount and as a percent of revenue. Look at your profits *in relation to something else* to adequately measure profitability, instead of just looking at the numbers.

INCOME STATEMENT ADJUSTMENTS

Some expenses on the income statement may not be all that business-related. The business may be paying above-market rent on a building that the business owner owns, as an example. Some employees may be above-market compensation or have expensive perks. Such expenses artificially reduce the profitability of the business and the resulting profit margins. It also may be appropriate to add back one-time expenses like repairs after a flood or extraordinary legal expenses in a lawsuit.

Your internally prepared income statement should *always* reflect straight-line depreciation to measure your profitability correctly, even though you reflect accelerated depreciation on your tax return. Ask your CPA for your depreciation schedule if you are unsure of the straight-line depreciation on your fixed assets.

You cannot change your income statement, but it may be appropriate to reduce some expenses to measure "normal" profitability

DURSON DISTRIBUTORS CASE STUDY

The following page represents the income statements for Durson Distributors for the last three years.

	20X1	% Rev	20X2	% Rev	20X3	% Rev
Revenue	$5,368	100%	$4,750	100%	$4,805	100%
Cost of goods sold	3,446	64.2	3,078	64.8	3,118	64.9
Gross profit	$1,922	35.8	$1,672	35.2	$1,687	35.1
Advertising	72	1.3	70	1.5	65	1.4
Bad debts	51	1.0	45	0.9	40	0.8
Depreciation	49	0.9	50	1.1	48	1.0
Equipment leases	17	0.3	16	0.3	18	0.4
Insurance	71	1.3	80	1.7	92	1.9
Legal and accounting	13	0.2	15	0.3	17	0.4
Miscellaneous	39	0.7	27	0.6	34	0.7
Office expense	29	0.5	33	0.7	32	0.7
Payroll tax and benefits	146	2.7	148	3.1	153	3.2
Rent	100	1.9	100	2.1	100	2.1
Repairs and maintenance	31	0.6	29	0.6	30	0.6
Salaries	520	9.7	528	11.1	560	11.7
Sales commissions	145	2.7	144	3.0	136	2.8
Business tax and license	27	0.5	25	0.5	31	0.6
Telephone and utilities	38	0.7	41	0.9	42	0.9
Travel and entertainment	21	0.4	24	0.5	33	0.7
Vehicle expense	73	1.4	88	1.9	90	1.9
Total operating expense	1,442	26.9	1,463	30.8	1,521	31.6
Operating profit	$480	8.9%	$209	4.4%	$166	3.5%
Other income	15	0.3	18	0.4	20	0.4
Other expense	(39)	(0.6)	(27)	(0.6)	(32)	(0.7)
Interest expense	(13)	(0.2)	(9)	(0.2)	(7)	(0.1)
Net profit	$443	8.4%	$191	4.0%	$147	3.1%

PROFITABILITY ANALYSIS

These are the gross profit margins for the last three years:

	20X1	20X2	20X3	Industry Average
Gross Profit Margin	35.8%	35.2%	35.1%	34.1%

The gross profit margin has been declining over the three years. Mr. Durson is probably not focusing on this profitability level, but he should determine why it has declined 0.7% during this period. That represents a loss in gross profit of $330k based on revenue in 20X3. Every dollar of that would have dropped to the operating profit if the gross profit margin had not declined, increasing from $166k to $496k. This is an excellent example of the importance of the gross profit margin's impact on the operating profit!

These are the operating profit margins for the last three years:

	20X1	20X2	20X3	Industry Average
Operating Profit Margin	8.9%	4.4%	3.5%	5.5%

The operating profit margin has declined because the gross profit margin has fallen, and indirect expenses have increased as a percent of revenue. Restoring this profit margin will require an examination of the gross profit and the indirect expenses. Every dollar of indirect expense should be examined to determine where cuts can be made.

These are the net profit margins for the last three years:

	20X1	20X2	20X3	Industry Average
Net Profit Margin	8.3%	4.0%	3.1%	4.7%

The net profit margin has declined significantly since 20X1 and is currently well below the industry average. Again, this decline is due to the increase in indirect expenses as a percent of revenue as well as a drop in the gross profit margin.

Mr. Durson has a solid balance sheet and the company is profitable, so he is probably comfortable. What is lacking is any focus on why the profit margins are declining. It would be fair to assume that Durson Distributors is in the plunder phase of business.

TIPS TO INCREASING PROFITABILITY

The economy goes up, and the economy goes down. We experienced the "Great Recession" in 2008, and many firms lost a lot of money. We had a 100-year event in 2020, and a lot of firms lost a lot of money. The following are six tips that will help you avoid losses and achieve sustained profitability in good and bad times.

ONE: ACT PROMPTLY

The first instinct when revenue and profits decline is to work harder. "Things are tough now, but they are going to get better, so what we need to do is sell more to generate more revenue." This strategy may work but betting the business on that is risky. Start cutting expenses immediately. Begin with the low-hanging fruit; travel, entertainment, cell phone allowances, free snacks in the lunchroom, etc. If losses persist, move to the next level like a 401k match and car allowances. If losses continue, proceed to laying off people. This is not pleasant, especially if they are long-term productive employees, but you need to do it.

The main thing is to not succumb to the "Things are going to get better" theory. Ultimately, they will, but it may be months. Act promptly to avoid losses and keep cutting costs until you restore profitability. Laying off employees is always painful but necessary. You owe it to the remaining employees to keep the business healthy.

TWO: ASK FOR HELP

Your leadership team and other employees know where you can save money, and you should ask them for suggestions. Determining how to operate more efficiently is not be a one-person activity. Your employees want the business to survive, and you should give them a chance to offer their suggestions.

THREE: AUDIT YOUR EXPENSES

Sit down with your bookkeeper or controller and look at *every dollar* that you spend. My experience is that this exercise usually results in a minimum savings of 10 percent. You can get complacent over time and consequently have unneeded expenses.

FOUR: AUDIT YOUR STAFF LEVELS

Look at every position in your company and satisfy yourself that it is a full-time job. Most are, but some may be able to be eliminated or combined with another position. All your employees may "look" busy, but remember the rule that w*ork expands to fill the time available.* Make sure that all your employees are actually busy.

FIVE: KNOW YOUR COSTS

Most business owners have only a vague idea of what it costs to provide a service or product. This lack of knowledge results in pricing that is at best haphazard, and at worst, follows what everyone else is doing (who are equally in the dark).

Dig into the details and make every effort to establish your product costs and then price according to the gross profit you want to achieve. Your competitors will probably increase their prices, and everyone will increase their profit margins.

SIX: THINK STRATEGICALLY

Jeff Bezos at Amazon says, "Every day is day one." Today's business environment is changing at warp speed, and you need to either change with the times or risk becoming obsolete.

Production workers are succumbing to robots. Print books are succumbing to E-readers. Brick and mortar retailers are succumbing to online sellers. Desktop computers are succumbing to laptops, which are succumbing to tablets, which are succumbing to plus-sized cell phones. Cameras and landline telephones are succumbing to cell phones.

Phonebooks, yellow pages, and encyclopedias have already succumbed to online information services. Hand-held maps have already succumbed to GPS devices. Grocery clerks will soon succumb to smart carts that pay automatically when you leave the store. Truck drivers will succumb to self-driving trucks.

Every day is day one. You need to pay close attention to your industry trends and change with the times or risk going out of business. Failure to adhere to some or all of the tips is why firms lack profitability, and following them is your insurance against low or nonexistent profits.

The highly profitable firms that I have observed over the last forty years make money regardless of the economy. Cutting expenses and letting people go is hard, but don't hesitate if it is necessary.

THE REST OF THE STORY

Oh, and now let me share with you all the things that we did to measure our consulting firm's profitability. The answer is simple, not very much. We had nice cash flow and no debt, so we looked at the income statement monthly to make sure we were adhering to the plan. We did *not* separate our direct and indirect expenses and therefore did not calculate a gross profit margin or cost out our services.

I am embarrassed to admit that. There are many things included in this book that I have learned since I sold that business, and if I had known them at the time, we would have been even more successful. I understand the temptation to avoid doing some of the necessary actions to sustain profitability is compelling. This is especially true if you are doing well and are not motivated to improve. Please don't succumb to that temptation. The message is, "do what I say and not what I did." You will be more successful as a result.

SUMMARY

There are three levels of profitability that you need to measure; gross profit margin (GPM), operating profit margin (OPM), and net profit margin (NPM)

A small percentage increase or decrease in the gross profit margin will significantly impact the operating and net profit margins. Therefore, the gross profit margin is the most important ratios that you will calculate. A decline of even 0.1 percent should be examined closely to determine the cause and the corrective action.

The income statement analysis for Durson indicates that the gross profit margin is declining, and indirect expenses are increasing, both in dollar amount and as a percent of revenue. This combination has significantly hurt profit margins.

Mr. Durson should carefully analyze all the expenses for the last three years to determine why profit margins are declining and what expenses to cut.

The analysis of the income statement is neither complicated nor time-consuming. Three ratios for measuring profitability are sufficient to give you a good idea about your income statement's strength, and three or four years indicate any significant trends.

Do not worry about the formulas for determining the three levels of profitability. *Business Mastery*, an Excel-based workbook, is available that will calculate these ratios for you automatically. Download it and other excellent complimentary workbooks from www.60minutecfo.com

The next chapter looks at some relationships that combine accounts from both the balance sheet and the income statement to measure your business's operating performance.

Keep it simple, and keep on paddling!

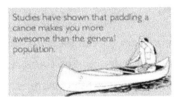

Studies have shown that paddling a canoe makes you more awesome than the general population.

CHAPTER THREE: OPERATING PERFORMANCE

3

INTRODUCTION

The previous two chapters have discussed relationships that are used to analyze the balance sheet and income statement. This chapter will discuss the six relationships that use accounts from each to measure operating performance. The six relationships are:

1. Return on equity
2. Receivable days (not needed for cash businesses)
3. Inventory days (not needed for service businesses with little or no inventory)
4. Payable days
5. Survival score
6. Revenue per administrative employee

RETURN ON EQUITY

Business owners often have a considerable sum of money invested in their businesses (defined as equity or net worth), and it is important to measure the return generated by the business to see how it compares to returns on investments available elsewhere that might be more diversified and less risky.

The formula for return on equity is:

$$\frac{\text{Net profit}}{\text{Equity}} \quad = \quad \textbf{Return on equity (ROE)}$$

Return on equity is an annual calculation, comparing the year's net profit to the ending equity. This calculation is performed once a year because the calculation of monthly or year-to-date return on equity ratios involves annualizing net profit. This annualized profit may not be representative of actual profitability, especially for a highly seasonal business.

RISK VERSUS REWARD

Return on equity is a measurement of the *reward* of owning a business, and it should be related to the corresponding *risk*. In chapter one, I described a company with a high debt-to-equity ratio as having high risk. Ideally, a high-risk company should have a high return on equity, i.e., more risk, more reward. The reverse is also true. Those companies with a very low debt-to-equity ratio or low risk will usually have a much lower return on equity.

High risk, high reward, and vice versa. Calculate your return on equity annually and compare it to your debt-to-equity ratio.

Twenty-five percent is a good standard for return on equity for most businesses.

RECEIVABLE DAYS

You do not want to have any more accounts receivable than is necessary for at least a couple of reasons. It hurts cash flow (more on that in the next chapter), and it is an asset that does not earn any return. Accounts receivable are essentially an interest-free loan to your customers. It is essential to calculate receivable days to ensure that it is within your company's guidelines.

Receivable days (also known as collection period, days sales outstanding, or DSO) is calculated in two steps:

$$\frac{\text{Revenue}}{\text{Accounts receivable}} \quad = \quad \text{Turnover}$$

$$\frac{\text{Period Days}}{\text{Turnover}} \quad = \quad \text{Receivable Days}$$

If this ratio is calculated for six months, use 180 for period days or 365 for one year. Always use the appropriate number of days in the period as the numerator in the second formula. These adjustments for the days in the period also apply when calculating inventory days and payable days.

AGING OF ACCOUNTS RECEIVABLE

In addition to calculating receivable days, you should get an aging of your accounts receivable every week. To age accounts receivable, separate them into categories based on their due dates:

Age	Expressed as
0 to 30 days	$ and % of total
30 to 60 days	$ and % of total
60 to 90 days	$ and % of total
Over 90 days	$ and % of total

Over sixty-day accounts should not be more than 10 percent of the total, and weekly monitoring of this aging will facilitate this process. This aging is significant to your banker, who will not typically use any accounts receivable over ninety days as collateral for your line of credit, thus restricting your borrowing limit.

Assign a person to collect delinquent accounts. Focus on the oldest ones first and make every attempt to collect this money. Those companies are paying someone, and it is the people who are calling them.

Minimizing your accounts receivable is essential from both a cash flow as well as a profitability standpoint. The older an account receivable is, the less likely you will be to collect it.

I will share the procedures at my company for controlling accounts receivable at the end of this chapter. Keep reading to learn "the rest of the story."

INVENTORY DAYS

You do not want to have any more inventory than is necessary for at least a couple of reasons. It hurts cash flow (more on that in the next chapter), and you want to avoid slippage and obsolescence. It is essential to calculate inventory days to ensure that it is within your company's guidelines. Obviously, this ratio is not needed for a service company.

Inventory days, the number of days it would take to sell all of the inventory is calculated in two steps as follows:

$$\frac{\text{Direct Expenses}}{\text{Inventory}} \quad = \quad \text{Turnover}$$

$$\frac{\text{Period days}}{\text{Turnover}} \quad = \quad \text{Inventory days}$$

Inventory turnover is the number of times that inventory turns over in a year. If inventory turnover is six times a year, as an example, it will turn over every 60 days, which we call "inventory days."

Some manufacturing firms reduce inventory requirements and thus increase inventory turnover (and increase cash flow) using a just-in-time inventory system. They require suppliers to deliver a part at the exact time when needed for production. In this fashion, manufacturers can reduce inventory requirements to minimize holding costs, maximize cash flow and increase profit margins.

Another technique used to reduce inventory is to have your vendors store inventory in your facility and charge you only as you use it. The goal is to have minimum cash tied up in inventory to maximize cash flow (more on managing cash flow in the next chapter).

PAYABLE DAYS

Accounts payable should be kept current. Late payments hurt your credit rating, can lead to a restriction of credit, and negatively impact your ability to borrow from the bank.

Payable days are calculated in two steps:

$$\frac{\text{Direct Expenses}}{\text{Accounts payable}} \quad = \quad \text{Turnover}$$

$$\frac{\text{Period days}}{\text{Turnover}} \quad = \quad \text{Payable days}$$

THE SURVIVAL SCORE

The Survival Score is based on the Z score that was used to predict bankruptcy. It was originally published in 1968 by Edward I. Altman. I have used it for the last 35 years and have determined it to be a good measure of the overall health of your business. Successful companies consistently have a Survival Score of more than 4.0. The ratings for the Survival score are as follows:

<2.0	Bad
2.0 – 2.9	Poor
3.0 – 3.9	Fair
4.0 – 4.9	Good
5.0 +	Excellent

The Survival Score is a combination of four ratios and a good measurement of your business's survival potential. Don't worry about calculating this ratio. **Business Mastery** calculates it for you automatically. If you would like to have the formula, please email me, and I will send it to you.

You should use 5.0 as a good standard.

REVENUE PER ADMINISTRATIVE EMPLOYEE

It is often difficult to determine if you have excess office staff. Therefore, it is advisable to check this from time to time by comparing your administrative employees to revenue.

Administrative employees are all office staff, including the CEO, and excluding commissioned salespeople. If you have employees that spend only part of their time with administrative matters, add up the part-time people to get a full-time equivalent.

Calculate this ratio comparing revenue to admin employees:

$$\frac{\text{Revenue}}{\text{Admin employees}} = \text{Rev. per admin employee}$$

Industry averages for this ratio do not exist, but it will be possible for you to determine a good standard for your business after measuring this for a few years.

This ratio does not imply that administrative employees generate a certain amount of revenue. This ratio is solely intended to help you determine the amount of revenue per administrative employee to determine an appropriate and efficient headcount for administrative employees. Use a full-time equivalent if you have part-time workers in this category.

CASE STUDY: DURSON DISTRIBUTORS

RETURN ON EQUITY

These are the return on equity ratios for Durson Distributors:

	20X1	20X2	20X3	Industry Average
Return on equity	50.6%	18.3%	12.5%	31.3%

Return on equity has declined over the last three years and is less than half of the industry average of 31.3 percent. This low return is a function of both declining profit margins and high equity. The debt-to-equity ratio is the *risk* measurement and return on equity is the *reward*. For Durson, the *reward* is low, as reflected by a low return on equity, but so is the corresponding *risk*, as indicated by the low debt-to-equity ratio of 0.36 in 20X3. Low risk, low reward.

RECEIVABLE DAYS

These are the number of days it would take to collect all the accounts receivables:

	20X1	20X2	20X3	Industry Average
Receivable days	41 days	46 days	39 days	37 days

Receivable days have improved slightly over the last three years and is in line with the industry average of thirty-seven days.

INVENTORY DAYS

These are the inventory days:

	20X1	20X2	20X3	Industry Average
Inventory days	49 days	53 days	58 days	60 days

Inventory days has increased over the three periods, which has hurt cash flow (more on this in the next chapter); however, the ratio for 20X3 is very close to the industry average of 60 days. This trend should be monitored and not allowed to worsen.

PAYABLE DAYS

These are the payable days (how long it would take to pay all the accounts payable):

	20X1	20X2	20X3	Industry Average
Payable days	48 days	43 days	35 days	41 days

Payable days have decreased over the three years and are better than the industry average of 41 days.

THE SURVIVAL SCORE

These are the Survival scores for the three years:

	20X1	20X2	20X3	Standard
Survival score	8.1	8.7	10.0	5.0

Durson Distributers is well above the standard and has excellent overall financial health.

REVENUE PER ADMINISTRATIVE EMPLOYEE

These are the revenue per administrative employees ratios:

	20X1	20X2	20X3	Standard
Rev. per admin. Emp.	$335.5	$296.9	$282.6	$300.0

Julian looked at these numbers and was dismayed to see that revenue per admin employee was steadily declining. He vowed that he would carefully examine each staff position to see if there was an ability to lay someone off or combine two positions into one.

He further determined that $300k looked like it might be a good standard to shoot for going forward.

THE REST OF THE STORY

Oh, and now let me share the procedures that we used to make sure that we collected our accounts receivable.

One morning at 8:30 am, my bookkeeper called me and said, "You might like to come down to my office." When I walked down the hall and entered her office, she said, "I thought you might be interested to know that for the first time in the history of the company, our over 90-day accounts receivable exceed $100,000." I looked at her in horror and said, "You're darn right I want to know that! Give me the list, and I will make some calls!"

When I got to the fifth one down the list, I was alarmed to see that it was one of my clients that owed us $6,500 that was over six months past due! When I called the bookkeeper of that firm, he immediately said,

"Oh, I was wondering when we were going to hear from you. The truth is, we are having a little cash flow problem, and the boss said not to pay any bills unless the people we owed called us." "Really?" I said. "Yup. I got the checks right here in my desk drawer, and I'm putting yours in the mail as we speak." "Really?" I said. "Yup, the check is in the mail." Sure enough, in three days, we got the check.

It is embarrassing to admit that we had no procedure for collecting past due accounts and were not paying any attention. We were way too busy teaching people how to manage accounts receivable!

After that experience, it was easy to sit down with our bookkeeper and controller and implement the necessary controls to keep this from happening again. Another lesson in sound financial management learned!

Like I said earlier, do as I say, not as I did!

SUMMARY

This chapter has discussed six ratios that utilize accounts from both your balance sheet and income statement. These ratios are not complicated and are a measure of various aspects of your operating performance.

In this and the previous two chapters, we have discussed a total of eleven ratios that measure liquidity, safety, profitability, and operating performance. These ratios tell us what we need to know about the balance sheet's strength, your profitability, and operating performance.

If there are ratios specific to your business or industry that are important to measure, you should add those to this list but avoid including dozens more. Too much information is worse than too little because it becomes difficult to focus on your business's most important areas.

Ensure that your leadership team members know these ratios and what they mean. If you have too many, it will make that task more difficult. Remember to keep it simple when analyzing your financial statements. More is not necessarily better. If you need to dig deeper into the details you can always do that.

Do not worry about the formulas for calculating any of these ratios. *Business Mastery*, an Excel-based workbook, is available that will calculate these ratios for you automatically. Download it and other valuable complementary workbooks from www.60minutecfo.com. Your assignment is to know these eleven ratios cold.

Cash is king. The next chapter will discuss how to measure and analyze cash flow.

Keep it simple, and keep on paddling!!

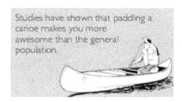

Studies have shown that paddling a canoe makes you more awesome than the general population.

CHAPTER FOUR: CASH FLOW

INTRODUCTION

Cash flow has always been an unknown to business owners. Prior to 1987, your CPA provided you with an annual "Source and Application of Funds" statement in addition to your balance sheet and income statement. It was never clear what "funds" meant, and this document was neither understandable nor something you could replicate in your firm.

In 1987 the accounting profession designed a more readable "Statement of Cash Flow," which contained three types of cash flow;

1. Operating Cash Flow
2. Investing Cash Flow
3. Financing Cash Flow

While an improvement over the Source and Application of Funds statement, it still suffered from being complicated and, worse yet, was not replicable in your business. The result was that you could neither measure nor forecast cash flow in your business on a regular basis, until now.

In 2017 I came up with formulas for Operating Cash Flow (cash flow from operations) and Financing Cash Flow (cash flow from owners and banks) that provide you with a statement of cash flow that you can use in your business every month.

Business owners work hard every day to increase revenue and net profit in the mistaken belief that they will have more cash if they have more profit. If only it was that simple. The fact is that profit has no relationship to cash flow. It is possible to have a profit and negative cash flow, or a loss and positive cash flow.

It is essential to measure cash flow because;

1. You pay your bills with cash,
2. You pay your people with cash,
3. You pay your debts with cash.

You don't pay anything with profit.

There are several reasons why business owners have had difficulty analyzing cash flow:

1. Cash flow is not consistently defined. If you ask five financial analysts for the definition of cash flow, you may get five different answers. This is not helpful.
2. Of the thousands of numbers on your monthly balance sheet and income statement, *not one pertains to cash flow.*
3. The statement of cash flow that you receive from your CPA once a year is difficult to understand, and you can't replicate it in your bookkeeping system.

"I can see my profits, but where is my cash?" is the plaintive cry of the business owner. This chapter answers that question.

TWO TYPES OF CASH FLOW

The two types of cash flow that I derived in 2017 are:

1. **Operating cash flow**: cash flow from the operations of the business.
2. **Financing cash flow**: cash flow from either banks or owners of the business.

OPERATING CASH FLOW

Operating cash flow is the cash flow generated from the day-to-day operations of your business. It consists of net profit (or loss) and changes in selected assets and liabilities from one period to the next. the formula is:

Net profit (loss)	plus
Change in current assets, excluding cash	plus
Change in current liabilities, excluding bank and shareholder debt	plus
Change in net fixed assets	plus
<u>Change in non-current assets</u>	**equals**
Operating cash flow	

FINANCING CASH FLOW

Financing cash flow consists of changes in bank debt, shareholder debt, and other long-term debt from one period to the next as follows:

Change in bank or lease debt	plus
Change in shareholder debt	plus
Change in other non-current debt	plus
<u>Equity adjustment</u>	**equals**
Financing cash flow	

Bank debt includes your line of credit (LOC), current portion of long-term debt (CPLTD), long-term bank debt, and capital leases reflected as a liability on your balance sheet. Other non-current liabilities consist of such things as a loan from an affiliate.

Equity adjustments result from either a distribution to shareholders, a contribution to equity by shareholders, or an adjustment to retained earnings made by your CPA. Distributions to shareholders are standard in an S corporation so that they will have money to make estimated quarterly income tax payments.

NET CASH FLOW

Net cash flow is the sum of operating and financing cash flow:

Operating cash flow   plus
Financing cash flow   **equals**
Net cash flow

THREE CASH FLOW RATIOS

There are three ratios that I use to analyze cash flow.

OPERATING CASH FLOW MARGIN – OPCFM

The OpCFM is calculated by dividing operating cash flow by revenue.

$$\frac{\textbf{Operating cash flow}}{\textbf{Revenue}} = \textbf{Operating cash flow margin (OpCFM)}$$

This ratio is similar to the operating profit margin discussed in chapter two, which compares operating profit to revenue. The difference is that this ratio measures *operating cash flow* instead of *operating profit* as a percent of revenue. This ratio may be positive or negative in any given period.

FINANCING CASH FLOW MARGIN (FINCFM)

The FinCFM is calculated by dividing the financing cash flow by revenue.

$$\frac{\textbf{Financing cash flow}}{\textbf{Revenue}} = \textbf{Financing cash flow margin (FinCFM)}$$

This ratio may be positive or negative in any given period.

NET CASH FLOW MARGIN (NETCFM)

$$\frac{\text{Net cash flow}}{\text{Revenue}} = \text{Net cash flow margin (NetCFM)}$$

This ratio may be positive or negative in any given period, but over time, *it must be positive* and my experience is that it is usually between 0.1 and 1.0 percent of revenue.

FINANCIAL STATEMENT IMPACT ON CASH FLOW

Factors from both the income statement and the balance sheet impact cash flow in your business. These factors can be either positive or negative per the following diagram.

Income Statement	Impact on Cash Flow	Balance Sheet
Net Profit ➔	POSITIVE ⬅	Assets Decrease Liabilities Increase
Loss ➔	NEGATIVE ⬅	Assets Increase Liabilities Decrease

POSITIVE CASH FLOW FACTORS

The positive contribution to cash flow from the income statement is net profit. Emphasis is on the word *contribution*. Net profit does not equal cash flow but does contribute to it.

The positive contributions from the balance sheet are a decrease in assets or an increase in liabilities. A reduction in accounts receivable generates positive cash flow. When assets go *down*, cash flow goes *up*. Obtaining a bank loan or increasing accounts payable also generates positive cash flow. When liabilities go *up*, cash flow goes *up*.

NEGATIVE CASH FLOW FACTORS

When assets go *up*, cash goes *down*.

If growth in revenue and net profit is significant, there will likely be an inverse relationship between profit and cash flow. This occurs because of the increase in assets caused by the increase in revenue.

EIGHT STEPS TO GROWING BROKE

1. A rapid increase in revenue causes a rapid increase in assets.
2. A rapid increase in assets causes a rapid decrease in cash.
3. A rapid decrease in cash causes a rapid increase in liabilities (accounts payable, bank line of credit, etc.).
4. A rapid increase in liabilities causes a rapid increase in the debt-to-equity ratio.
5. A rapid increase in the debt-to-equity ratio causes a rapid increase in the risk of the business (see chapter one).
6. A rapid increase in the risk of the business causes the bank to be nervous.
7. An increase in the nervousness of the bank causes loan availability to be shut off.

8. Shutting off loan availability ensures that the business will not have sufficient capacity to fund growth (without an injection of capital), which precipitates a crisis with unpaid creditors.

Business owners have a hard time understanding why the availability of loans is cut off by the bank when the company is growing and profitable. "Stop it," says the banker. "Stop growing revenue and profits? Why in the world would I do that?" responds the bewildered business owner.

The answer lies in understanding the impact of rapid growth on negative cash flow and the increase in the debt-to-equity ratio. The problem is cash flow, not profit. The fact is that *no one* can grow as fast as they want. The goal is to understand that and figure out an acceptable rate of growth by making financial projections. Monitoring and projecting your financial ratios and cash flow utilizing ***Business Mastery*** make this easy!

ANALYZING CASH FLOW

Negative cash flow is not necessarily bad. It could be caused by a growth spurt in revenue and increased profits. When revenue goes up, assets go up, and cash goes down.

Positive cash flow is not necessarily good. It could be caused by not paying your accounts payable (when liabilities go up, cash goes up).

The solution is to analyze cash flow in the context of your other key financial indicators. If your eleven ratios outlined in chaptes one and two look okay, then your negative or positive cash flow is okay. Always remember, however, that net cash flow *must be positive in the long term.*

Measure your financial ratios and cash flow every month utizing *Business Mastery,* . and always remember that cash is king.

CASE STUDY: DURSON DISTRIBUTORS

OPERATING CASH FLOW

Account	20X1	20X2	20X3
Net profit	$443	$191	$147
Change in current assets[1]	8	22	31
Change in current liabilities[2]	(3)	(109)	(60)
Change in net fixed assets	6	25	40
Change in noncurrent Assets	(4)	(2)	5
Operating cash flow	$450	$127	$163

[1] Excluding cash.

[2] Excluding bank/lease debt and shareholder debt.

Current assets went down all three years, resulting in cash going up by a total of $61k. Current liabilities went down in all three years resulting in a reduction in cash of $172k. Net fixed assets went down in all three years resulting in cash going up by $41k. Noncurrent assets went up by $6k and down by $5k resulting in cash going down by $1k.

Study the above table and make sure you understand what the positive and negative numbers mean. When assets go *down*, cash goes *up,* and when liabilities go *down*, cash goes *down*.

OPERATING CASH FLOW MARGIN

	20X1	20X2	20X3
$450 ÷ revenue of $5,368 =	8.4%		
$127 ÷ revenue of $4,750 =		2.7%	
$163 ÷ revenue of $4,805 =			3.4%

FINANCING CASH FLOW

Account	20X1	20X2	20X3
Change in bank/lease debt	($50)	($58)	($30)
Change in shareholder debt		-0-	-0-
Change in other long-term liabilities		-0-	-0-
Equity adjustment	(387)	(21)	(17)
Financing cash flow	(437)	($79)	($47)

Financing cash flow is negative for all three years. When liabilities go *down*, cash flow goes *down*. Negative financing cash flow means that debt is being paid.

FINANCING CASH FLOW MARGIN

		20X1	20X2	20X3
($437) ÷ revenue of $5,368	=	(8.1%)		
($79) ÷ revenue of $4,750	=		(1.7%)	
($47) ÷ revenue of $4,805	=			(1.0%)

NET CASH FLOW

Account	20X1	20X2	20X3
Operating cash flow	450	127	163
Financing cash flow	(437)	(79)	(47)
Net cash flow	$13	$48	$116

NET CASH FLOW MARGIN

	20X1	20X2	20X3
Operating cash flow margin	8.4%	2.7%)	3.4%
Financing cash flow margin	(8.1%)	(1.7%)	(1.0%)
Net cash flow margin	0.3%	1.0%	2.4%

Durson had strong operating cash flow in all three years and used part of that cash to pay off debt. The remainder was added to cash on hand. You can see that cash flow for the three years was strong.

RELATIONSHIP BETWEEN CASH FLOW AND PROFIT

There is rarely any relationship between profit and cash flow as reflected by the following for Durson Distributors:

	20X1	20X2	20X3	Total
Operating profit	$480	$209	$166	**$855**
Operating cash flow	$450	$127	$163	**$740**
Net profit	$443	$191	$147	**$781**
Net cash flow	$13	$48	$116	**$177**

You can see that there is *no* consistent relationship between profit and cash flow. Always analyze cash flow in the context of your overall financial health as measured by the eleven financial ratios.

BUSINESS MASTERY WORKBOOK

Do not worry about the formulas for calculating operating and financing cash flow or the three cash flow ratios. *Business Mastery* calculates these for you automatically. Download it at www.60minutecfo.com.

OTHER TYPES OF CASH FLOW

There are two other types of cash flow with which you should be familiar. One is daily cash flow, and the other is seasonal cash flow.

DAILY CASH FLOW

       Ending cash from the previous day

Plus: Accounts receivable collections

         Cash receipts

         Investment income

Minus: Accounts payable payments

         Loan/lease payments

         Payroll payments

         Other expenses payments

Equals **Ending cash for the current day**

If you have a cash flow problem in your business, you should estimate daily cash flow for at least thirty days ahead so that you can schedule when you be able to make payments to creditors. Make a point to communicate with them so that they know you are working on this and that you intend for them to be paid.

SEASONAL CASH FLOW

Many businesses are seasonal, which dramatically impacts cash flow during the year. Accounts receivable grow along with revenue (when assets go *up*, cash goes *down*) per the following diagram.

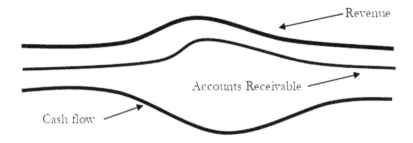

Jan Feb Mar April May June July Aug Sept Oct Nov Dec

As accounts receivable go *up* in the peak season, cash flow goes *down*, causing a need for a seasonal bank line of credit. As revenue and accounts receivable decline at the end of the season, cash flow is positive, allowing for the credit line's repayment.

DIVERSIFICATION

Note what happens in the diagram below if you can diversify and reduce the seasonality of your business. Cash flow does not go down but builds nicely throughout the year. The company is more profitable and saves interest expense because there is little or no need for a line of credit.

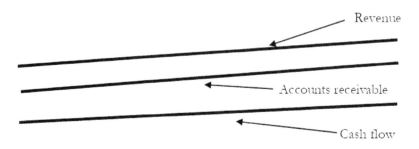

Jan Feb Mar April May June July Aug Sept Oct Nov Dec

Include diversification in your long-term business strategy if possible to avoid losing money or having negative cash flow several months a year.

EIGHT TIPS FOR MAXIMIZING CASH FLOW

These are steps that you can take to maximize cash flow in your business.

1. Collect your accounts receivable on a timely basis. Get an aging of your accounts receivable every week and have someone regularly call the accounts over 60 day accounts. No more than 5 to 10 percent of your total accounts receivable should be in the over-sixty-day category.
2. Invoice promptly. You cannot collect money until you send an invoice to the customer.
3. Diversify into non-seasonal lines of business if possible. This will reduce the seasonality of your business and help cash flow on a year-round basis.
4. Manage growth carefully. A high growth rate in revenue causes growth in assets, which creates negative operating cash flow.

5. Borrow as long-term as possible. Payments are lower, thus helping cash flow, and you can always pay the loan off sooner if justified by cash flow.

6. Never use short-term sources of cash like a line of credit to fund a long-term asset. Always use a long-term source of funds for this.

7. Maximize your net profit *margin*. Get as much bang for your revenue buck as you can.

8. Minimize the purchase of fixed assets. Rent in the short term, or lease assets with no down payment whenever possible to conserve cash.

A summary of the financial analysis for Durson Distributors is on the following page.

SUMMARY OF DURSON DISTRIBUTORS FINANCIAL ANALYSIS

	20X1	20X2	20X3	RMA	Comment
Liquidity					
Current ratio	2.38	2.97	3.89	1.60	Good and getting better
Safety					
Debt equity ratio	0.77	0.49	0.36	1.70	Good and getting better
Survival score	8.3	8.8	10.2	N/A	Good and getting better
Profitability					
GPM	35.8%	35.2%	35.1%	34.1%	OK but declining
OPM	8.9%	4.4%	3.5%	5.5%	Poor and declining
NPM	8.3%	4.0%	3.1%	4.7%	Poor and declining
Operating Performance					
Ret. on equity	50.6%	18.3%	12.5%	31.3%	Poor and declining
Receivable days	41	46	39	37	OK and getting better
Inventory days	49	53	58	60	Good but increasing
Payable days	48	43	35	41	Good and getting better
Rev/admin emp.	$356	$297	$283	N/A	Declining
Cash flow					
OpCFM	8.4%	2.7%	3.4%	N/A	Positive
FinCFM	(8.1%)	(1.7%)	(1.0%)	N/A	Negative – paying off debt
NetCFM	0.3%	1.0%	2.4%	N/A	Positive and getting better

OBSERVATIONS ARE EASY TO SEE:

1. Liquidity is strong.
2. Safety is strong.

3. Overall, the balance sheet is strong and getting stronger.
4. Profitability is poor and declining.
5. Return on equity is poor and getting worse, although this is commensurate with the low level of risk as indicated by the low debt-to-equity ratio.
6. Receivable days are declining and close to the industry average, indicating good accounts receivable management.
7. Inventory days are good but increasing and should be watched.
8. Payable days are good and getting better.
9. The Survival score is excellent and getting better.
10. Revenue per admin employee is declining.
11. Operating cash flow margin is strong.
12. Financing cash flow margin is negative, indicating the repayment of debt.
13. Net cash flow margin is positive every year and getting better.

SOLUTIONS FOR DURSON DISTRIBUTORS

Calculating eleven ratios and looking at the trends has told us the following:

1. Liquidity and safety are strong, probably better than necessary.
2. Cash flow is strong.
3. It is easy to see that profitability needs work. It is poor and declining.

The gross profit has been in decline, and the most probable reason for that is failing to increase prices when costs have increased. The solution is to increase revenue, not decrease direct expense.

Indirect expenses have increased as a percent of revenue which is always a bad sign, but Julian is comfortable and complacent in his plunder phase. He needs to sit down with his controller and go over every indirect expense line item and identify what has caused the increase and if it's necessary. It is a matter of focus, first on the gross profit margin and secondly on the indirect expenses.

This may take a little time, but it is not complicated. He may determine that the bulk of the increase is because he has long-time employees that get a raise every year and are likely paid more than the market rate for their position. Or he may see that he is spending too much on advertising or entertainment just because that's what they have always done.

The examination of the gross profit margin and the indirect expenses will be sufficient to restore this business's profit margins.

There is nothing complicated about this analysis. We looked at fourteen key relationships that measure liquidity, safety, profitability, operating performance, and cash flow. *Learning* what these ratios measure is not difficult but *remembering* what they measure is problematic. You can only accomplish this by monthly repetition. You need to use **Business Mastery** to calculate these ratios every month and remind yourself what they mean and measure. Refer back to these chapters once a month.

Fourteen ratios tell it all, not twenty or thirty. Keep working at it until you know them cold. Share them with your leadership team and make sure that they understand them as well. You teach what you want to learn.

Give this analysis 60 minutes a month, and in a short period, you will be at a point where there is no mystery at all about business finance. You and every manager in your company will know what success looks like and what you need to do to be successful. This knowledge is very powerful.

BUSINESS MASTERY

Do not worry at all about the formulas for any of these ratios. *Business Mastery*, an Excel-based workbook, is available on www.60minutecfo.com, that does these calculations for you automatically.

SUMMARY

It is crucial for you to know and understand your operating and financing cash flow and whether they are positive or negative. Measure and understand your cash flow, and you will join a very select group of business owners who understand the difference between profit and cash flow.

This chapter concludes our discussion of the fourteen ratios that measure your financial strengths and weaknesses. Go back and scan these chapters once a month. The only way you will thoroughly learn and internalize these ratios is to use them regularly to help you manage a successful and profitable business. Refer to Appendix IV for a summary of these ratios. Make copies of that page for your leadership team and refer to it monthly.

The numbers on your income statement and balance sheet do not tell you the whole story concerning your financial condition and may even be misleading. You need to look at *key relationships* to understand and determine your financial condition.

Think about what these ratios measure and why you are calculating them. Set standards for these ratios, and then manage your business accordingly. When you master an understanding of these relationships, you will join the elite 5 percent of business owners who understand the financial dynamics of their business.

Business finance, taken step-by-step, is neither difficult nor complicated. If any, problems are easy to spot, and solutions are almost always apparent.

HOMEWORK ASSIGNMENT

Do not calculate any ratios or cash flow by hand. It is not a good use of your time and ***Business Mastery***, an Excel-based workbook, is available to do it automatically. Download it from www.60minutecfo.com, and input the last three to five year-end financial statements and monthly financial statements for the current year.

Ask your banker or CPA for a copy of the Risk Management Association (RMA) ratio averages for your industry and put those in the appropriate column on the end of year ratios tab. This information is also available by request on my website www.60minutecfo.com.

Study the ratios and cash flow, look at the trends over the years, and see how you compare to the RMA industry averages. Determine what areas of your business are financially strong and those areas that need improvement. Share and discuss this information with your leadership team. If you have questions about the analysis, ask your CPA for assistance.

Use *Business Mastery* to prepare a forecasted income statement and balance sheet for the current year, as discussed in chapters 7 through 10. If the resulting forecasted ratios and cash flow are not healthy, revise the forecasts until they are. Refer to chapter thirteen on how you should use this information in communicating with your banker. If you do this, you will a very small number of bank customers that do anything remotely like this, and your relationship will become much more substantial.

The next chapter will describe how your income statement, balance sheet, and cash flow all interact.

Keep it simple, and keep on paddling!

CHAPTER FIVE: BRINGING IT ALL TOGETHER

5

INTRODUCTION

Three years ago, a friend of mine, Chuck Feinstein, told me that I needed to produce a graph of how the balance sheet, income statement, and cash flow all interacted. As a nuclear physicist, he was excited to read about business finance, but he wanted a graphical representation of how it all interacted. I told him it would be nice to have such a thing, but there were just too many moving parts, and I couldn't do it. He nagged me until I relented and sat down to see if I could do it, expecting to prove to him that it wasn't possible.

I did it, and the result is what you see on the next page. For every cause, there is an effect. Everything is interrelated, and you can see how by studying this diagram. Check it out on the following page.

FINANCIAL ANALYSIS CAUSE & EFFECT DIAGRAM©

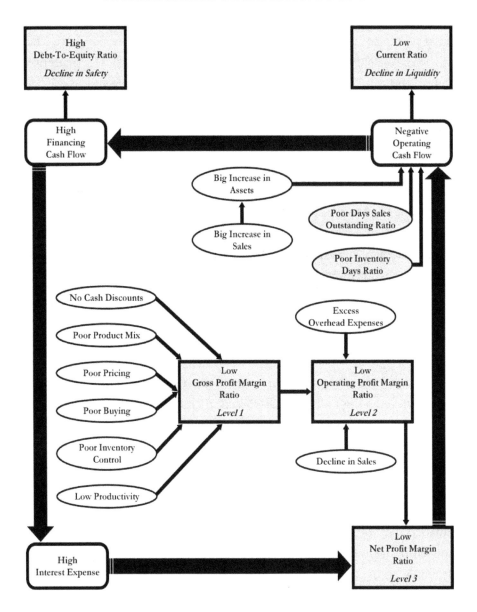

Using the diagram is easy. Start at the lower right-hand corner with Low Net Profit Margin and work to the left to see causes, and up the right-hand side to see effects. The arrow's tip is always the effect, and the base of the arrow is the cause. Take a few moments to study it. Go from box to box and think about what is a cause and what is an effect.

Sir Isaac Newton once said:

> *When one body exerts a force on a second body, the second body simultaneously exerts a force equal in magnitude and opposite in direction on the first body.*

That Isaac was a smart dude. When you do something in one area of your business, it impacts many other areas.

The lower half of the diagram contains the income statement and the three profitability levels discussed in chapter two.

The upper third of the diagram contains cash flow, both operating cash flow and financing cash flow discussed in chapter four.

At the very top is the balance sheet reflecting liquidity and safety, as discussed in chapter one.

I was understandably proud of this achievement, but Chuck was not satisfied. He wanted me to discuss the concept of optimization because he instinctively knew that maximizing or minimizing anything was probably an oversimplification and not theoretically correct. The guy is a real nag, but I agreed to give it a shot.

SEEK TO OPTIMIZE, NOT MAXIMIZE

If liquidity is good, then more is better. If safety is good, then more is better. If revenue growth is good, then more is better. These statements sound right, but they are not. You need to determine what is *optimal* for your business and not seek to maximize or minimize anything. *Optimize* is your goal.

OPTIMAL LIQUIDITY

The current ratio, which measures liquidity, is important (see chapter one), but a higher ratio is not necessarily better than a lower ratio. A ratio of 2.00 is very good, 3.00 isn't necessarily *better*, but it is *more liquid*.

A high current ratio with a high cash position is not necessarily desirable. Cash, even if it is invested in a CD or money market fund, produces a very low return. Cash that is not needed in the business should be distributed to owners who can invest it more profitably. If the business needs cash in the future, it can always be loaned back to the business with interest being paid to the owner. Another disadvantage is the fact that a lot of cash sitting on the balance sheet is a welcome target by an aggressive attorney if the company is hit with a lawsuit.

If you want to pay every bill when you receive it instead of in 30 days, you will need a high current ratio. Determine the amount of liquidity that is optimal for your company and then keep it there. Working capital is essential, and well-run companies pay their bills when they are due, but excessive liquidity is not necessarily desirable.

OPTIMAL SAFETY

Safety, the ability to withstand adversity, is important. Adversity can strike at any time, and you want to be able to survive. The debt-to-equity ratio measures safety and the lower this ratio is, the safer you are.

That does not necessarily mean that a lower ratio is better, but it is *safer*. A ratio of 1.00 is good. That would mean $1.00 in debt for every $1.00 in equity. The creditors have the same amount invested in the business, as does the owner. At least four factors are going to dictate the optimal degree of safety for your business:

1. Personal risk tolerance.

If your parents always taught you that debt is bad and borrowing is something to avoid, you will be less tolerant of risk. Also, risk tolerance is likely to change with age and personal circumstances. At age sixty-five, you are more concerned about preserving your assets than you were at age thirty-five. If you have six kids, a mortgage, and college expenses to plan for, you probably will be more risk-averse than a young single person with no debt and no kids.

2. Type of industry.

Some industries are more leveraged than others. Automobile dealers or other businesses that borrow to invest in their inventory have debt-to-equity ratios that are routinely 4.00 or higher. Motels and other real estate type businesses have high debt-to-equity ratios because their assets are mortgaged. Restaurants, particularly those that are newly established, tend to have higher debt-to-equity ratios. It is one of the reasons that you see these types of businesses failing when there is a downturn in the economy. It is not because restaurants are *inherently* riskier types of businesses; they may have a high debt-to-equity ratio at the time of the adversity.

Automobile dealerships, motels, and restaurants that have been established for many years and have paid off a lot of their debt are the ones that are the most likely to survive.

3. State of the economy.

If the economic indicators are favorable and all the economic forecasts are good, it may be a time to grow the company and take on more debt (and risk) in the process. On the other hand, if economic forecasters are beginning to talk about a potential economic downturn, this information may indicate that it is time to reduce debt to improve safety.

4. The phase of business.

New companies in the wonder and blunder phases of business have more risk and higher debt-to-equity ratios than more established businesses in the thunder and plunder phases. It goes with the territory. The good news is that most companies survive those early days by a combination of hard work, determination, sweat equity, and maybe a little luck.

More than 80 percent of businesses fail in the first ten years, but the causes of those failures tend to be bad management rather than a high debt-to-equity ratio.

OPTIMAL PROFITABILITY

Some would say that it is impossible to be too rich or too thin, and you probably think that this includes profitability—it does not. Chapter five illustrates what can happen to a business that pursues revenue growth and higher profits without any notion of the company's overall financial condition. If some profit is good, that does not necessarily mean that more profit is better.

Also, there are ways to maximize profitability that may be harmful to the business. Hiring cheap labor, working them hard, and frequently turning them over will increase profits in the short-term but probably hurt in the long-term. Failing to maintain equipment or cutting advertising and marketing budgets will increase profit in the short-term and have undesirable long-term consequences. Sometimes lower profitability may be beneficial. There are times when you must invest and increase expenses to make more money down the road.

Optimal profitability is unique to your situation. It is going to be determined by measuring the gross, operating, and net profit margins (see chapter two) and establishing what they *should* be based on a combination of several factors:

1. What your profit margins have been historically
2. The profit margins of others in your industry
3. The condition of your industry
4. The condition of the economy
5. The amount of competitive pressure you face
6. Your pricing strategy—high cost, low volume versus low cost, high volume, etc.
7. Supply and demand
8. Current fads

You need to be profitable, and you should strive to determine your optimum profit margins within the context of the above factors. Then you need to faithfully track your profit margins and strive to keep them at the level that you have determined to be appropriate.

WHY YOU SHOULD BOTHER WITH ANY OF THIS

There are approximately 28 million small businesses (defined by the SBA as having 500 or fewer employees) in the United States, and if only 2 percent are aware of the contents of this book, that means that 27.4 million of them are not doing much in the way of financial analysis. Since they seem to be doing okay, you might be wondering why you should bother with this. Several reasons come to mind:

1. They are all *not* doing okay. 80 to 85 percent of them fail within the first ten years of their existence. Many of those that don't fail are, at best, mediocre in their performance. Their owners are working for a paycheck and not building anything of value.

2. Unless you practice good leadership and calculate the key relationships outlined in this book regularly, you will be unlikely to achieve excellence.

3. Owning and operating a business is a life-long learning exercise. The people who get this right are the ones who are willing to never stop learning and growing and never believe that they "know it all." They are always asking questions and then listening to the answers. They are real students of the game, and they are successful, stimulating, and enjoyable to be around. Strive to be one of them!

SUMMARY

This book is about looking at a few financial relationships so that you can understand where you have been and, more important, give you an idea as to where you are going.

Financial management is neither complicated nor time-consuming, but it does take some effort on your part. Having just read the last five chapters, it is all fresh in your mind, and you now have a basic understanding of what to do and how to do it. But if you put this book down and never refer to it again, this information will soon be lost. Stay with it. Give it 60 minutes a month. That is the only way that it will become ingrained in your thinking.

Business Mastery allows you to see areas needing improvement quickly, and in most instances, the solutions are apparent. An 80 percent failure rate within ten years of being in business should be enough of a motivator. If most of those business owners had invested 60 minutes a month as outlined in this book, the chances are excellent that they would still be in business. Think about the jobs and money lost, and the heartache and disappointment of failure that was avoidable.

Study this book, and the odds are that you are not going to fail, and better yet, you will run an excellent company and be sufficiently profitable. Provide this book to your leadership team, and make sure they all understand it as well. You will more successful if everyone is paddling in the canoe!

Above all, think about *optimizing* relationships rather than maximizing or minimizing them. Look at your historical performance, consider your personal feelings and beliefs, and establish your optimal numbers. It is common sense, and you do not need a degree in finance to do this.

Business Mastery, an Excel-based workbook, is available that you should use every month to determine how you are doing per plan. Download it at www.60minutecfo.com.

Success is not pre-destined, but it is certainly possible. Read this book regularly. Give it 60 minutes a month - less than one percent of your time. It is a small investment that will pay big dividends!

The next chapter will describe what happens when dad retires, and the son takes over.

Keep it simple, and keep on paddling!

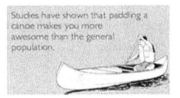

CHAPTER SIX: THE NEXT GENERATION

6

INTRODUCTION

Julian Durson spent most of his life building a solid business with $2.4 million in revenue, and he was well-respected in the community. He was the past president of his trade association, the downtown Rotary Club, and the Pleasant Hills Golf and Country Club, where he is currently on the board of trustees.

Dad is happy with the current situation, but his son Allen has a different opinion. He has seized on this analysis to renew his efforts to get dad to retire and let him take over. The sales staff is ancient, tired, and unproductive, profits are moribund, growth is nonexistent, and the competition is eating their lunch. It will not be long, in his not-so-humble opinion, before they lose many of their major accounts to more aggressive competitors. It is easy for him to see that things are in dire straits, and he is at a loss to understand why dad does not agree.

In desperation, he enlists the aid of his mom Sara, who has been after Julian for several years to spend more time at their Florida condominium. Allen's arguments play right into her desires for the future, and she is a willing ally in trying to convince Julian to retire and enjoy the fruits of his hard labor.

After several weeks of debate, Julian finally agrees to head south with Sara and let Allen take over the business.

THE NEW PRESIDENT

Allen arranged for all but one of the sales staff to retire gracefully, hired a new VP of sales, and three new salespeople. He hired a firm to update the marketing brochures and website, assigned sales territories, and set aggressive sales goals for the salespeople.

He had his eye on two promising locations in neighboring states and immediately searched for potential sites for new branches. He was making sure that Durson Distributors would not be left behind in the economic expansion that the industry was currently experiencing.

His work and planning were rewarded by significant revenue growth, which averaged nearly 40 percent per year. By the end of 20X6 revenue was over $6 million, more than twice the revenue in 20X3. He took the entire sales staff and their families on a four-day cruise to the Bahamas to reward their hard work. Allen was pleased with himself, and morale in the company was off the charts.

Amid all this celebrating, things were not quite so congenial at the bank. Allen financed this growth primarily with bank debt, and the once solid balance sheets did not have quite the luster that they had under Julian. Conversations with the banker became increasingly strained, and this was baffling to Allen. Both revenue and operating profit had doubled in a short three-year period, and he thought that everyone should be singing his praises. Instead, the banker was making noises about restricting loans to the company going forward.

Dad was not too pleased either when Allen asked him to loan the company money in 20X5 and 20X6. He was lulled into acceptance by the glowing reports he received from Allen, but could not understand why he had to put money into the company if things were going so well.

The balance sheets for the period 20X1 to 20X6 are on the following page.

	Julian Years			Allen Years		
	20X1	20X2	20X3	20X4	20X5	20X6
Cash	$154	$202	$318	108	$90	$104
Trade accounts receivable	601	595	510	845	1,325	1,999
Inventory	463	445	497	978	1,560	2,601
Other current assets	37	39	41	55	84	101
Current assets	$1,255	$1,281	$1,366	$1,986	$3,059	$4,805
Gross fixed assets	862	887	895	1,301	1,789	2,100
Accumulated depreciation	(602)	(652)	(700)	(768)	(888)	(1,068)
Net fixed assets	260	235	195	533	901	1,032
Other assets	35	37	32	44	52	55
Total assets	$1,550	$1,553	$1,593	$2,563	$4,012	$5,892
Line of credit-bank	-0-	-0-	-0-	194	773	1,436
Trade accounts payable	451	359	300	560	888	1,619
Accrued expenses	38	21	20	45	66	97
Curr. Port. L-T bank debt	39	52	31	55	102	118
Current liabilities	$528	$432	$351	$854	$1,829	$3,270
Long-term bank debt	147	76	67	423	683	947
Shareholder debt	-0-	-0-	-0-	-0-	100	150
Total liabilities	$675	$508	$418	$1,277	$2,612	$4,367
Equity	$875	$1,045	1,175	$1,286	$1,400	$1,525
Total liabs. and equity	$1,550	$1,553	$1,593	$2,563	$4,012	$5,892

Allen looked at these balance sheets and observed that total assets and equity were up every year, and concluded that things were looking good. For his life, he could not understand why the bank had a problem, and he seriously considered looking around for another bank that would be more appreciative of the progress that he has made as president of the company.

Allen looked at the numbers, but let's look at the relationships that measure liquidity and safety and see how the balance sheets are performing.

LIQUIDITY—ALLEN

		Julian			Allen		Industry
	20X1	20X2	20X3	20X4	20X5	20X6	Average
Current ratio	2.38	2.97	3.89	2.23	1.67	1.47	1.60

Liquidity has declined dramatically from 20X3 to 20X6. A current ratio of 1.47 means that the company has $1.47 in current assets to pay $1.00 of current liabilities. Liquidity is marginal and rapidly declining.

SAFETY – ALLEN

	Julian			Allen			Industry
	20X1	20X2	20X3	20X4	20X5	20X6	Average
Debt-to-equity	0.77	0.49	0.36	0.99	1.87	2.86	1.70
Survival Score	8.3	8.8	10.2	6.2	4.2	3.3	N/A

A quick look at the increasing debt-to-equity ratio is enough to see why the banker is alarmed. Safety has deteriorated badly since 20X3, and the debt-to-equity ratio is much higher than the industry average. A debt-to-equity ratio of 2.86 means that the company has $2.86 in liabilities for every $1.00 of equity. In other words, the creditors have almost three times more invested in the business than the owner does. The higher the debt-to-equity ratio, the less safe the company is and the more nervous the banker.

The Survival Score, a measure of the business's overall health, has declined from a strong 10.2 (anything over 5.0 is excellent) to a very marginal 3.3 in just three years.

Assets are up, and equity is up. The *numbers* tell us that the balance sheets are good and getting better, but the *ratios* tell us that they are terrible and getting worse.

This example illustrates the benefit of monthly calculating your financial ratios. Your accounting system provides you with monthly financial statements (the numbers), but not the ratios. It is safe to say that Allen was not calculating these ratios regularly.

PROFITABILITY—ALLEN

Liquidity and safety are declining. The balance sheet is marginal and getting worse. Let's look at the following page to see how the income statements are doing.

	Julian Years			Allen Years		
	20X1	20X2	20X3	20X4	20X5	20X6
Revenue	$5,368	$4,750	$4,805	$6,555	$9,177	$13,100
Cost of goods sold	3,446	3,078	3,118	4,274	6,048	8,725
Gross profit	$1,922	$1,672	$1,687	$2,281	$3,129	$4,375
Advertising	72	70	65	89	125	180
Bad debts	51	45	40	64	81	95
Depreciation	49	50	48	70	95	126
Equipment leases	17	16	18	30	61	88
Insurance	71	80	92	110	150	201
Legal and accounting	13	15	17	25	31	33
Miscellaneous	39	27	34	35	46	81
Office expenses	29	33	32	48	55	71
PR tax and benefits	146	148	153	200	281	412
Rent	100	100	100	187	210	325
Repairs and maint.	31	29	30	22	36	31
Salaries	520	528	560	735	1,039	1,480
Sales commissions	145	144	136	172	236	393
Business tax and lic.	27	25	31	35	60	72
Tel. and utilities	38	41	42	48	47	52
Travel and Ent.	21	24	33	65	95	147
Vehicle expenses	73	88	90	109	152	201
Total indirect expenses	1,442	1,463	1,521	2,044	2,800	3,988
Operating profit	$480	$209	$166	$237	$329	$387
Other income	15	18	20	19	21	28
Other expenses	(39)	(27)	(32)	(40)	(55)	(51)
Interest expense	(13)	(9)	(7)	(47)	(109)	(175)
Net profit	$443	$191	$147	$169	$186	$189

Allen looks at these numbers and feels more than vindicated. He set out to increase revenue and profit, and that is precisely what he has done. All his hard work over the last three years has paid off handsomely, and he is already scouting out another location for expansion in 20X7 or 20X8.

The *numbers* reflect that revenue has grown dramatically, and operating profit in 20X6 is almost twice what it was in 20X3, but the *relationships* tell us that profitability is in free-fall. The 1.4 percent net profit margin in 20X6 is the lowest that the company has ever experienced. The numbers are up, but the profit margins are down.

These are the three profit margins for the last six years:

| | Julian | | | | Allen | | Industry |
	20X1	20X2	20X3	20X4	20X5	20X6	Average
GPM	35.8%	35.2%	35.1%	34.8%	34.1%	33.4%	34.1%
OPM	8.9%	4.4%	3.5%	3.6%	3.6%	3.0%	5.5%
NPM	8.3%	4.0%	3.1%	2.6%	2.0%	1.4%	4.7%

The cause of the decline in profitability is easy to see. The gross profit margin has declined from 35.8 percent to 33.4 percent. This drop in the gross profit margin plus the increase in interest expense has caused a considerable reduction in the net profit margin.

OPERATING PERFORMANCE: ALLEN

So far, we have observed declining liquidity, safety, and profitability by calculating five key ratios, and these problems were not at all difficult to spot. Now let's look at the operating performance ratios under Allen's leadership.

		Julian			Allen		Ind.
	20X1	20X2	20X3	20X4	20X5	20X6	Aver.
Return on equity	50.7%	18.3%	12.5%	13.1%	13.3%	12.4%	31.3%
Receivable days	41	46	39	47	53	56	37
Inventory days	49	53	58	84	94	109	60
Payable days	48	43	35	48	54	68	41
Survival score	8.1	8.7	10.0	6.1	4.1	3.3	N/A
Rev. per admin emp.	$335	$296	$282	$252	$241	$229	N/A

Return on equity (reward) has continued to decline and is considerably less than the industry standard of 31.3 percent. Since the debt-to-equity ratio has gone up dramatically, this means that the company has more *risk* and less *reward*, precisely the opposite of what you want to happen.

Receivable days have ballooned up in the last three years, and this has sucked up precious cash (when assets go up, cash goes down). This increase directly results from opening two new branches and not paying attention to collecting accounts receivable. Inventory days have ballooned up from 49 to 109 for the same reason.

Payable days are over 60 because the company now lacks working capital, and the creditors are not pleased.

Revenue per administrative employee has steadily declined under Allen's leadership.

Operating performance is poor under Allen's leadership. Now let's look at cash flow.

CASH FLOW: ALLEN

OPERATING CASH FLOW

The following is the operating cash flow for six years.

	Julian			Allen		
	20X1	20X2	20X3	20X4	20X5	20X6
Oper. cash flow	450	127	163	(726)	(932)	(915)
OpCF Margin	8.4%	2.7%	3.4%	(11.1%)	(10.2%)	(7.0%)

Revenue has gone up dramatically, causing assets to go up dramatically, causing operating cash flow to go down dramatically—a lot of drama and a lot of stress. Cash flow from operations is negative in all three years.

Dad may have been conservative and unwilling to take many risks, but he did generate positive operating cash flow and reduce debt. In the last three years of his stewardship, the company made $855 in operating profit and had positive operating cash flow of $740 (450+127+163). Perhaps this did not set the world on fire, but it was not so bad either.

In the period since Allen has taken over, the company made $953 in operating profit and had negative operating cash flow of $2,573 (726+932+915) —good profits but terrible cash flow!

FINANCING CASH FLOW

The following is the financing cash flow for six years:

	Julian			Allen		
	20X1	20X2	20X3	20X4	20X5	20X6
Fin. cash flow	(437)	(79)	(47)	516	814	929
FinCF Margin	(8.1%)	(1.7%)	(1.0%)	7.9%	10.0%	7.1%

Dad paid off $563 in debt (437+79+47), and son managed to get the company $2,259 deeper in debt (516+814+929).

As you can imagine, both the banker and dad were not at all pleased about this, and both demanded corrective action. Take note that the increase in debt was *not* the problem per se; it was an increased debt-to-equity ratio with the corresponding drop in safety that was the source of trouble. Put yourself in the shoes of the banker, and you can see why she was not happy.

Operating cash flow has gone from positive in the Julian years to dramatically negative in the Allen years. Increased revenue caused assets to go up, which caused a decrease in operating cash flow. As assets go *up*, cash goes *down*. You can picture in your mind what one or two more years of this kind of "success" will look like for Durson Distributors. The bank will shut off loans, demand repayment, and the company may have to go out of business. It's called *growing broke*.

Financing cash flow has gone from negative in the Julian years (debt was reduced), to positive in the Allen years (debt was increased). Allen has used a combination of bank, trade, and shareholder debt (none of which was his money) to fund the growth of the company. He felt justified in doing this because the company was so "successful" under his leadership.

Ratios for the Julian and Allen years are the following:

	Julian years			Allen years		
	20X1	20X2	20X3	20X4	20X5	20X6
Liquidity						
Current ratio	2.38	2.97	3.89	2.33	1.67	1.47
Safety						
Debt-to-equity	0.77	0.49	0.36	0.99	1.87	2.86
Survival score	8.1	8.7	10.0	6.2	4.2	3.3
Profitability						
Gross profit margin	35.8%	35.2%	35.1%	34.8%	34.1%	33.4%
Operating profit margin	8.9%	4.4%	3.5%	3.6%	3.6%	3.0%
Net profit margin	8.3%	4.0%	3.1%	2.6%	2.0%	1.4%
Operating Performance						
Return on equity (ROE)	50.6%	18.3%	12.5%	13.1%	13.3%	12.4%
Receivable days	41	46	39	47	53	56
Inventory days	49	53	58	84	94	109
Payable days	48	43	35	48	54	68
Rev. per admin employee	$335.5	$296.9	$282.6	$252.1	$241.5	$229.8
Cash Flow						
Operating cash flow margin		2.7%	3.4%	(11.1)	(10.2%)	(7.0%)
Financing cash flow margin		(1.7%)	(1.0%)	7.9%	10.0%	7.1%
Net cash flow margin		1.0%	2.4%	(3.2%)	(0.2%)	0.1%

The problems in 20X6 are easy to spot:

1. Liquidity at 1.47 is marginal and getting worse.
2. Safety at 2.86 is terrible and getting worse.
3. Profitability at 1.4% is terrible and getting worse.
4. Return on equity at 12.4% is terrible and not commensurate with the risk as reflected by the increased debt-to-equity ratio.
5. Receivable days at 56 are terrible and getting worse.
6. Inventory days at 109 are terrible and getting worse.
7. Payable days at 68 are terrible and getting worse.
8. The Survival score at 3.3 is marginal and declining rapidly.
9. Operating cash flow is negative for all three years.
10. Revenue per employee is steadily declining, probably indicating excessive office staff.
11. The debt-to-equity ratio has gone up, and the safety of the company has deteriorated. The bank is not pleased

MEETING AT THE BANK

The banker saw these problems, even if Allen did not, and at her insistence, Julian flew up from Florida for a meeting with Allen in the bank's conference room. The banker said that she was alarmed at the company's liquidity and safety deterioration and announced that the bank would not provide any additional loans. She further demanded that existing loans be paid down sufficiently so that the debt-to-equity ratio would be under 2.00.

Allen was offended and defensive at this demand, and Julian was apoplectic. His signature was on the personal guarantees, and he could easily visualize his nest egg evaporating. He was in a vicious mood, and he could not imagine how he was going to explain to Sara that their comfortable lifestyle was in peril if this situation could not be salvaged.

The banker was fearful about her loans and upset that the long-time relationship with Durson Distributors was deteriorating. Dad was fearful and upset about the business's deteriorating state and the stability of his financial situation. Allen was upset and angry about being criticized for what he believed to be a spectacular performance.

THE PLAN

After a lot of heated discussions, they decided to pursue the following course of action:

1. Allen would cease all efforts to grow revenue, work on generating positive operating cash flow, and abandon any plans to open another branch.
2. A temporary person would be hired immediately to work on collecting past-due accounts receivable to no more than forty receivable days by the end of March. Proceeds would be applied to bank debt.
3. Allen would carefully analyze the inventory and reduce inventory days to no more than forty-five by the end of February. Slower moving items would be moved at a discount if necessary.
4. There would be an immediate freeze on hiring and raises until further notice.
5. Allen would come up with a plan for laying off staff if it became necessary.

6. Cash generated from the reduction in the assets mentioned above (as assets go *down,* cash goes *up*) would go first to reduce bank debt and then to reduce accounts payable if any was available. No payment would be made on the loan of $150 to Julian without permission from the bank in writing.

These efforts were forecasted to generate over $2 million in operating cash flow to reduce bank debt. The banker agreed to continue to finance the operations on a day-to-day basis, with the stipulation that the line of credit would be paid off no later than the end of April.

Allen didn't like any of this, but when faced with complying with this plan *or else,* he finally agreed. He recognized this as a near-death experience, and he wanted to appease dad and keep his job. He was skeptical that this could be accomplished in such a short time, but he promised to do his best.

This plan took a little longer than expected, as plans often do, but Julian, who willingly put golf on the back burner, helped Allen, and they were able to get Durson Distributors back on a firm footing by the end of six months. The banker was keenly interested in the process and carefully monitored the progress in reducing bank debt.

UNDERSTANDING BUSINESS FINANCE

Julian and Allen both eventually realized that this crisis did not need to happen in the first place. If *anyone* at Durson Distributors had been calculating the financial ratios regularly, the problems would have been spotted well in advance to allow for corrective action. The reality is that, even if they had been calculated, no one at Durson Distributors would have understood what the ratios meant. Management believed that more revenue and profits were good, *no matter what.* This belief proved incorrect, and this was easy to see by looking at a few relationships.

THE NEW PHASE OF BUSINESS

Julian guided Durson Distributors successfully through the wonder, blunder, and thunder phases and wound up contentedly in the plunder phase. Allen correctly realized that the company needed to grow and yanked the business directly back into a blunder phase. He was revenue-driven. If some revenue is good, more is better. Well, maybe not.

LESSONS LEARNED

Julian was happy in the plunder phase, and Allen was determined to blunder. Both were incorrect, and three years of high growth under Allen took the company to the brink of insolvency.

Both learned that with even a cursory glance, a few relationships would have avoided the entire issue. Problem areas would have been easy to spot in time for corrective action.

I urge you to download the **Business Mastery** workbook and use it to calculate these ratios monthly. Keep this book handy on your credenza and re-read chapters one through four describing financial ratios every month. Keep paddling in these waters until you know instinctively and intuitively where you are and where you are going. Remember this principle:

What gets measured gets managed, and what gets managed gets fixed.

This analysis is not complicated; it is simple. Be sure to visit www.60minutecfo.com and download *Business Mastery* that will make these calculations for you automatically. While you are there, describe your industry and I will send you the RMA ratio averages that apply to your company.

SUMMARY

Julian Durson founded a company at the age of thirty-four and worked hard over the years to build it into a sound and profitable company.

When Julian retired at the end of 20X3, the company was safe, liquid, profitable, and had positive cash flow. It was solidly in the plunder phase of business, and Julian could not find anything about which to be unhappy. Life was good, and he was especially pleased that his son Allen had decided to join the company as the successful director of sales.

Dad was comfortable, and his son was frustrated. He wanted dad to grow the business. Dad always responded by saying, "Sure, son, that's something we could consider." but then he did absolutely nothing. When Allen, in desperation, enlisted mom's help in getting dad out of the way, the momentum began to shift. Allen set out to grow the company without any restraint, and the rest is history.

All the pain that came later could have been avoided by calculating fourteen simple ratios regularly, but that did not happen. Allen was a salesperson, not a finance person.

Allen knew what to do and how to do it and entered a new business blunder phase with a vengeance. Revenue skyrocketed, and cash flow plummeted. Interested parties like the banker and trade creditors began to get less and less cordial, just when everyone should have proclaimed him businessman of the year. All this culminated in a very emotional meeting in the bank's conference room.

It is easy to see how that meeting could have been avoided. You simply need to look at a few key relationships. *Business Mastery*, an Excel-based workbook, is available for downloading at www.60minutecfo.com. Get it and use it monthly. Avoid a contentious meeting in your bank's conference room!

Do you want to grow fast? Be careful what you wish for. Growth is good, but you need to manage it carefully. The ratios will help you do this. Focus on what Julian had accomplished versus what Allen's strategy achieved. Using *Business Mastery* every month will ensure that this does not happen to you.

The next chapter will describe the planning process in detail, an essential aspect of success that is rarely done.

Keep it simple, and keep on paddling!

Studies have shown that paddling a canoe makes you more awesome than the general population.

CHAPTER SEVEN: INTRODUCTION TO BUSINESS PLANNING

7

INTRODUCTION

It is unwise to operate a business without a plan, without any idea what you are trying to achieve or where you are going. It is akin to navigating in unknown waters without a chart—you never know where you might end up. Despite this, most business owners resist planning. They tend to be action-oriented, and the task immediately before them is what gets their attention. In my experience, less than five percent of all businesses take the time to do any planning whatsoever.

FOUR REASONS WHY BUSINESS OWNERS DON'T PLAN

ONE: THEY DON'T KNOW HOW TO DO IT

It takes effort and a lot of thought to put together a business plan, and you may not know how to start. This chapter describes the steps involved in generating a strategic and financial plan for your business.

TWO: THEY DON'T HAVE TIME

The biggest excuse I hear is lack of time. "You don't understand, Dave. I am already working ten to twelve hours a day, six or seven days a week, struggling to succeed in this business. The phone is always ringing. When am I supposed to find time to plan?" I understand that concern from first-hand experience, but the answer is that in the long run, planning doesn't *take* time; it *saves* time. Instead of answering the same questions over and over, you answer them once. With a plan, you become *proactive* instead of *reactive*. Your efforts are more productive and efficient, giving you *more* time to devote to your day-to-day activities.

THREE: FEAR

Fear of the unknown. Fear of being held accountable. Fear of not making your plan. When you commit to a plan on paper, others can see it. They will know if you don't achieve it. They may be critical of your performance. Who needs this? It's less stressful not to commit yourself in the first place.

Good leaders don't mind being held accountable. They understand that a written plan enhances communications with your leadership team and ensures that everyone is on the same page, working to achieve common goals. Courage is one of the attributes required to succeed in business, which means doing something even though you are fearful.

FOUR: UNCERTAINTY

The business environment has changed a lot in the past few years, and it promises to change even more in the future. With the uncertainty that such changes bring, why bother to put together a plan? It is just going to be obsolete quickly anyway.

On the contrary, facing an uncertain future is a significant reason to establish strategies, set goals and objectives, and develop a sound business plan.

WHY PLANNING IS IMPORTANT

Benefits include:

1. Encouraging management to consider and evaluate necessary company policies.
2. Encouraging management to look ahead, to consider conditions that are likely to prevail outside the company.
3. Promoting a team concept within the company.
4. Outlining the most effective and economical use of labor, facilities, and capital.
5. Enabling understanding throughout the company of the problems faced by each department.
6. Providing a means of evaluating progress or lack thereof toward stated goals.
7. Establishing a commitment to a plan of action.

8. Instilling in management the habit of carefully considering all factors before making a final decision.
9. Avoiding costly mistakes or errors in judgment.
10. Maintaining the focus of the employees on the stated mission and objectives of the business.

RESULTS OF NOT PLANNING

The lack of planning is often the cause of either serious problems or outright failure. Poor planning is estimated to account for over 90 percent of business failures. If you take it one step at a time, you will learn how to develop a business plan and begin to reap the substantial benefits listed above.

A diagram of the planning process is on the next page.

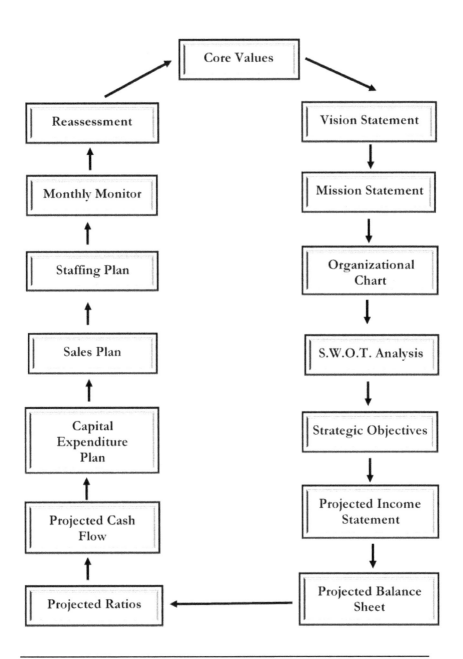

CORE VALUES

The planning process starts with the determination of the core values of the business. What values drive your company? What does the company stand for? Once you have established your core values, make sure your employees know what they are. Put a plastic card in a stand on every employee's desk. Post them in the conference room, lunchroom, and warehouse. Talk about them in staff meetings. These values define who you are, and these are the values that you want and expect your employees to follow.

I will share my experience with core values in my company at the end of this chapter. Keep reading to learn "the rest of the story."

I will share my experience with core values in my company at the end of this chapter. Keep reading to learn "the rest of the story."

VISION STATEMENT

The only thing worse than being blind is having sight and no vision.
Helen Keller

The Vision Statement is what you expect the business to look like at the end of two or three years. It can include the amount of expected revenue, the number of locations, services or products offered, etc. Once your management team has created your vision statement, post it in your lobby, conference room, lunchroom, and warehouse. Prominently display it where your employees can see it every day and make sure you discuss it in staff meetings and with all new employees so that they will know what your vision is, where you are trying to go, and how they can best help you get there.

At the end of 20X6, Durson Distributors will have revenue in excess of $6 million and be operating in two states and three locations.

MISSION STATEMENT

The mission statement should be a concise one or two-sentence statement that reflects the business's main purpose or focus. It answers questions like:

1. Why does the business exist?
2. What does the business do?

Once you have your mission statement done, post it in your lobby, conference room, lunchroom, and warehouse. Make sure it is prominently displayed where your employees and customers can see it every day. It does not have to be lengthy. The company I founded had a one-sentence mission statement:

We help businesses achieve financial success.

It was one sentence that explained why the company existed. It took two days to write it.

ORGANIZATIONAL CHART

Most business owners do not like to prepare a formal organizational chart because they want reporting relationships to be flexible and not tied down to lines and boxes. I started my business with eight employees and did not have an organizational chart because I wanted the flexibility of assigning tasks to anyone that was available. That is okay for a small start-up business, but it is necessary to establish more formal reporting relationships as the business grows.

Draw up an organizational chart if you have multiple reporting layers. Make sure everyone understands who reports to who, especially if there are dual reporting relationships (someone reporting to two different people). Ideally, no person has more than or six or seven direct reports, and review it at least annually to ensure it is up to date.

STRATEGIC PLANNING

Most businesses don't do strategic planning but ignore it at your peril. Today's business environment is changing at warp speed, and you need to determine how best to react to that changing environment.

Strategic planning anticipates future trends in the general business environment and your industry in particular. Firms like Boeing that build airplanes have to visualize the future demand for aircraft eight to ten years in advance, but most businesses have a two to three-year strategic planning horizon.

Updating your assessment of the overall business environment on at least an annual basis allows you to fine-tune your long-term strategies continually. Use a SWOT (**S**trengths, **W**eaknesses, **O**pportunities, **T**hreats) analysis to assess your business's external and internal environments.

The external environmental analysis determines the opportunities and threats and examines the following areas:

1. The competition
2. Legal/regulatory changes
3. The economy
4. The industry
5. Social trends
6. Emerging technology

Good business strategies take advantage of the opportunities and do everything possible to minimize the threats.

The internal environment analysis determines the strengths and weaknesses and examines the following items:

1. Personnel capabilities
2. Physical capacity
3. Financial capacity
4. Products/services offered
5. Sales and marketing
6. Organizational structure

Good strategies take advantage of the strengths and opportunities and do everything possible to avoid the threats and strengthen the weaknesses.

STRATEGIC OBJECTIVES

Setting strategic objectives is the next step, and they might be set in the following areas:

1. The growth rate for revenue or profits
2. Diversification plans
3. Updating systems, procedures or equipment
4. Acquisition or divestiture plans
5. Market share
6. Implementing new programs, services or products

The objectives should be clear, specific, realistic, flexible, measurable, controllable, have deadlines, and assigned accountability, such as:

Objective: Establish a plan for increasing the sales leads generated by the website.
Assigned to: Frank Anderson.
Deadline: May 1.

Avoid vague or immeasurable objectives like "be the best" and make sure that you monitor these objectives regularly.

Monitoring is a key phase of the planning process. Do not put the plan on the shelf and forget about it until the end of the year. Nothing will happen, people will think you were not committed to the plan, and you will have wasted a lot of time and effort.

FINANCIAL FORECASTS

Forecasting your income statement, balance sheet, ratios, and cash flow are described in the next chapters. Use *Business Mastery* to accomplish these forecasts.

CAPITAL EXPENDITURE PLAN

Business Equipment, an Excel-based workbook, is available to download on www.60minutecfo.com to assist in the capital budgeting process.

SALES PLAN

What are the sales goals? Who? How? When?

STAFFING PLAN

What staff will be either added or laid off? When?

MONTHLY MONITOR

Sit down every month with your leadership team and determine how the company is performing compared to the plan. Get explanations from key people or departments who are not performing as agreed. Make sure they are held accountable.

REASSESSMENT

The only constant in business is change. Nothing remains the same. Look at your strengths, weaknesses, opportunities, and threats at least annually. Reassess the overall direction of your business in light of the changing environment. Refine your vision, mission, goals, and objectives. Make sure you involve the key people in your company in this process so that they are committed to helping you achieve the plans for the business.

PLANNING TIMETABLE

The following is a timetable for the planning process. If your fiscal year-end is not December, your timetable will begin and end in different months.

September: Begin to assemble information on the economy and the industry for the coming year. Ask your bank, trade association, and CPA for help. Pay attention to what the forecasts are for the economy in general and your industry in particular.

October: Ask your salespeople for their estimates on what they think they can do next year. Look at your numbers at the end of September and begin to formulate a revenue forecast for the coming year.

November: Take your key management off-site to discuss and formulate your strategic and preliminary financial plan.

December: Revise and update your financial forecasts for the coming year based on your November financial statements.

January: Finalize your strategic and financial plan for the year after you have reviewed your in-house December financial statements.

THE REST OF THE STORY

Oh, and now let me share my experience with core values in my business. Our core values were displayed in the office's foyer, and all employees walked past them when entering or leaving. I assumed that they were familiar with them, but just to make sure, I asked if anyone could name them all in a monthly staff meeting. Not one of the 30 present could. I took a twenty-dollar bill out of my wallet and said, "whoever can name them all at the next staff meeting gets this $20."

Several raised their hands at the next meeting, and I awarded the money, and I kept that up until everyone earned the reward. I had to bribe my employees to know our core values, but I wanted them to know they were important. I urge you to have core values and to ensure then that everyone knows what they are.

SUMMARY

Business owners seldom take the time to plan. The phone is always ringing, and it's easy to be consumed by the pressures of the tasks at hand.

The fact is that planning does not *take* time; it *saves* time. You make decisions and set a course of action once instead of repeatedly. You are proactive instead of reactive. Invest the time and effort into this process, and your business will become more successful. *Writing it down is halfway there.*

There are some essential aspects of the planning process:

1. Make sure the managers who will be responsible for achieving the plan are involved in planning and are committed to the plan. Owners should not dictate the plan on a top-down basis.

2. Do not have your planning meeting at the company if at all possible. There are too many distractions. Go off to a hotel or resort. Ensure everyone has their computers and phones turned *off* and that they do *not* check e-mail or voice mail during the meeting or at breaks. If necessary, they can check for messages and return calls after the end of the day.

3. Try to include a social aspect to the meeting like a cocktail hour or meal. Give your employees a chance to interact on a non-business basis and get to know each other better. These people are the team that will help you achieve success, and the better they know, like, and respect each other, the more successful you will be.

4. It is often useful to have an outside facilitator assist in this process, especially when discussing your strengths and weaknesses. Seek out a business consultant for help and advice about this.

5. Review the progress of the plan monthly. Your plan is a dynamic description of what you hope to achieve, and it is not something

that should sit on your credenza until the end of the year. Establishing a plan and then ignoring it is worse than not having any plan at all (which is very bad).

Business Mastery, an Excel-based workbook, is available to assist you in making your financial forecasts. Be sure to download it at www.60minutecfo.com.

Refer to Appendix II for the outline of a Business Plan.

The next chapter will describe how to forecast the income statement.

Keep it simple, and keep on paddling!

CHAPTER EIGHT: FORECASTING THE INCOME STATEMENT

$$8$$

INTRODUCTION

Projecting the income statement is a four-step process.

1. Forecast revenue.
2. Forecast gross profit.
3. Forecast indirect expenses.
4. Forecast net profit.

FORECAST REVENUE

Factors to consider:

1. The status of the economy (national/local)

2. The status of the industry
3. Input from salespeople and key management
4. Historical revenue trends
5. Competition
6. Market size and share
7. Financial resources
8. Human resources
9. Physical resources
10. Anticipated changes in technology
11. Regulatory environment
12. Customer preferences/social trends
13. Management and employee input

A good thing to do is make three forecasts for revenue, which I call the 5-8-5 plans.

1. Worst case   5 out of 10 probability
2. Most likely   8 out of 10 probability
3. Best case   5 out of 10 probability

Complete the income statement and balance sheet forecasts for each scenario using **Business Mastery** and save each forecast. You will be in a good position to cut expenses as needed to minimize or avoid losses if you see that revenue is trending toward the worst-case assumption.

FORECAST GROSS PROFIT

Gross profit is equal to:

Revenue
(direct expenses)
Gross Profit

The gross profit is often forecasted based on a percentage of revenue. This gross profit percentage should reflect the historical margins as well as the goal for the coming year. Suppose you have established a standard within your company for the gross profit margin. In that case, multiply the forecasted revenue by the gross profit margin percentage to determine the gross profit.

You can also forecast gross profit by making a detailed forecast of each of your direct expenses. This type of detailed forecast is more time consuming and may or may not produce a more accurate result than applying a percentage to your forecasted revenue but should be considered if you plan to add or eliminate services or products in the coming year. Use the method, which is the simplest and produces the best results.

A third option to forecast the gross profit is as follows:

1. Project revenue.
2. Project indirect expenses that are needed to support that level of revenue.
3. Add 9.0% of revenue (if that is your goal for an operating profit margin) to the indirect expenses.

The dollar amount in step 3 produces the amount of gross profit needed to pay all indirect expenses and have a 9.0% operating profit margin. Divide the gross profit in step 3 by revenue, and you will know what your gross profit margin *should* be to give you a 9.0% operating profit margin. The challenge then is to determine if that gross profit is realistic based on historical performance.

FORECAST OPERATING PROFIT

Operating profit is equal to:

Revenue

(direct expenses)

Gross profit

(Indirect expenses)

Operating profit

Forecast indirect expenses individually on a line-by-line basis. Items such as bad debts or sales compensation may be forecasted based on a percentage of revenue. Administrative salaries should be forecast based upon projected headcount and whether you intend to grant any salary increases.

ZERO BASED BUDGETING

Do not simply start with the previous total assuming that it is the correct amount. Start from zero with each indirect expense and increase the amount according to your perceived need based on the revenue forecast.

FORECAST NET PROFIT

Net profit is equal to:

> Revenue
>
> (direct expense)
>
> **Gross Profit**
>
> (indirect expense)
>
> **Operating profit**
>
> other income
>
> (other expense)
>
> (interest expense)
>
> **Net profit**

Other income and other expense is forecasted based on historical experience, and interest expense is estimated based on borrowing forecasts and changes, if any, in interest rates.

CASE STUDY—DURSON DISTRIBUTORS

Allen and his leadership team spent a productive day in a planning meeting outside the business. It was the first-ever planning meeting for the company, and it started with an overview of the strengths, weaknesses, opportunities, and threats that Durson faced (SWOT analysis). This discussion turned out to be a spirited and candid assessment, and some members of the team had to be reminded occasionally not to take things personally. The result was a gradual increase in the feeling of camaraderie and team spirit as the day progressed.

The CFO then reviewed the financial results for 20X4—20X6 and talked about areas of the business that needed to improve. The VP of sales was particularly taken aback upon hearing some of this information, having felt that the increase in revenue under his leadership was nothing short of phenomenal. It took some time and convincing before he could understand that excessive growth may not be the best strategy from a financial standpoint.

After lunch, Allen spent time discussing the economic and industry conditions that they could expect in 20X7, and that was followed by a discussion of the potential revenue for 20X7. The consensus was that revenue growth in 20X7 should be planned at a maximum of 10 percent, which produced revenue of $14,400. The plan was to be selective and focus on higher-margin jobs. Jim Closing, the VP of sales, was not that enthusiastic about this strategy, but he ultimately agreed.

The group then turned their attention to expenses. It was decided that the gross profit margin would be improved to 34.0 percent, which was slightly less than what the company had experienced in 20X4. This gross profit margin produced a gross profit of $4,896 when multiplied by revenue. This was admittedly a conservative estimate considering previous higher gross profit margins, but Allen wanted a number that he was confident could be achieved.

They then spent the rest of the afternoon examining every operating expense in detail and determined where cuts and efficiencies could be obtained. There was a lot of spirited discussions back and forth as people attempted to protect their favorite expenditures, but in the end, everyone was surprised and pleased that they arrived at a 0.9 percent decrease over 20X6, despite the 10 percent forecasted increase in revenue. That would mean operating expenses of $3,952 and an operating profit of $944, or 6.6 percent.

The CFO then estimated other income, other expenses, and interest expense totaling ($85) which produced a net profit of $859. This net profit represented a net profit margin of 6.0 percent, the highest margin achieved in over ten years.

The leadership team felt proud of what they had accomplished. They had worked hard, learned a lot, and felt closer as a team. They knew what they hoped to accomplish in the coming year, and they were all committed to making it happen. Cocktails and a nice dinner allowed for a relaxing end to the day, and the attendees went home inspired and motivated to have a great year. The forecasted income statement for 20X7 is reflected on the following page.

	20X4	20X5	20X6	Planned 20X7
Revenue	$6,555	$9,177	$13,100	$14,400
Cost of goods sold	4,274	6,048	8,725	9,504
Gross profit	$2,281	$3,129	$4,375	$4,896
Advertising	89	125	180	170
Bad debts	64	81	95	101
Depreciation	70	95	126	115
Equipment leases	30	61	88	88
Insurance	110	150	201	221
Legal and accounting	25	31	33	30
Miscellaneous	35	46	81	75
Office expenses	48	55	71	68
P.R. tax and benefits	200	281	412	439
Rent	187	210	325	325
Repairs and maint.	22	36	31	35
Salaries	735	1,039	1,480	1,410
Sales commissions	172	236	393	432
Business tax and license	35	60	72	81
Tel. and utilities	48	47	52	45
Travel and entertainment	65	95	147	115
Vehicle expenses	109	152	201	202
Total operating expense	2,044	2,800	3,988	3,952
Operating profit	$237	$329	$387	$944
Other income	19	21	28	30
Other expenses	(40)	(55)	(51)	(40)
Interest expense	(47)	(109)	(175)	(75)
Net profit	$169	$186	$189	$859

SUMMARY

Projecting the income statement is the first step in the financial planning process. If you have multiple locations, each branch income statement should be forecasted, with the participation of the branch manager, and then combined for the overall company's income statement.

There is usually a lengthy, emotional, and largely unproductive debate about allocating administrative overhead to each branch. My advice is not to do this. Each branch manager should be held accountable for the revenue and direct branch expenses and the resulting branch gross profit that contributes to paying the company overhead. That is all that they can control, and it is what should be their focus.

Of course, each branch needs to contribute to the company operating expenses, but the overall profitability of the company is the responsibility of the business owner and leadership team, not the branch manager. I know that few business owners will agree with this, but the allocation of the company operating expenses to a branch will always be arbitrary and perhaps not that relevant.

Forecasts of the balance sheet, cash flow, and financial ratios are dependent upon the forecasted income statement and are discussed in the following chapters. Commit these plans to paper, and then monitor them every month during the year. In this fashion, both you and your key managers will be able to assess the progress towards achieving your financial goals.

When you incorporate a planning meeting and financial forecasting into your management process, you'll develop teamwork and the financial discipline needed to anticipate and assess your future performance.

Most businesses do not prepare a formal plan, despite the significant benefits derived from this exercise. If this includes you, pledge that you will make this happen in your company. Your employees want to help you achieve your company's goals, and they, therefore, need to be aware of what they are. Better yet, they should participate in establishing them. Nothing builds commitment like involvement.

Remember this:

The more you sweat in planning, the less you bleed in profits.

Business Mastery, an Excel-based workbook, is available to assist you in easily making your financial forecasts. Be sure to download it at www.60minutecfo.com.

The next chapter will discuss how to forecast the balance sheet.

Keep it simple, and keep on paddling!

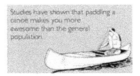

CHAPTER NINE: FORECASTING THE BALANCE SHEET

9

INTRODUCTION

The next step in the financial planning process is to forecast the balance sheet, the foundation of your business. The goal is to forecast numbers that will be reasonably close to actual results, given the revenue and profit forecasts. In other words, there is no need to try to get it down to the exact dollar. What you want is a reasonably close approximation of the balance sheet accounts so that you can forecast cash flow and the financial ratios. Feel free to round to the nearest thousand.

FORECASTING ASSETS

Cash is a plug number based on the minimum cash desired in the business. Put in any amount that you feel is appropriate.

Prepaid expenses and other current assets are forecasted as a percent of revenue.

Accounts receivable are forecast based on the desired receivable days.

Fixed assets are forecast based upon the capital expenditures planned for the year.

Accumulated depreciation is obtained from the depreciation schedule provided by the CPA.

Other assets are forecasted based on the business owner's knowledge of the assets that are contained in this category.

Summary of balance sheet account forecasting

Asset Accounts	Method
Cash	A plug amount
Accounts Receivable	Receivable days
Inventory	Inventory days
Prepaid expenses	Percentage of revenue
Other current assets	Percentage of revenue
Gross fixed assets	From capital expenditure plan
Accumulated depreciation	From depreciation schedule

Other assets   Based on account contents

FORECASTING LIABILITIES

The bank line of credit is forecasted last and will be an amount that is necessary to balance the balance sheet. *Business Mastery* does this for you automatically.

Accounts payable are forecast based on the number of payable days.

Accrued expenses and other current liabilities are forecast based on their percent of revenue.

The current portion of long-term debt and long-term debt are on the loan schedule provided by the CPA.

Other long-term liabilities are forecast based on the business owner's knowledge of the liabilities that are in this category.

Summary of forecasting Liability Accounts

Account	Method
Line of credit	Balancing number if needed
Accounts payable	Payable days
Accrued expenses	Percentage of revenue
Other current liabilities	Percentage of revenue
Current portion of long-term debt	Loan schedule
Long-term debt	Loan schedule
Other long-term liabilities	Based on account contents

FORECASTING EQUITY

Equity is forecast by adding forecasted net profit to the prior year's equity, less distributions to owners, plus contributions from owners.

Beginning equity
    Plus forecasted profit
    Minus distributions to owners
    Plus contributions by owners
    Equals
Ending equity

The forecasted balance sheet for 20X7 is on the following page.

The following is the forecasted balance sheet for Durson Distributors.

	20X4	20X5	20X6	Planned 20X7
Cash[1]	$108	$90	$104	$100
Accounts receivable[2]	845	1,325	1,999	1,381
Inventory[3]	978	1,560	2,601	1,510
Other current assets[4]	55	84	101	115
Current assets	**1,986**	**3,059**	**4,805**	**3,106**
Gross fixed assets[5]	1,301	1,789	2,100	2,100
Accumulated depreciation[6]	(768)	(888)	(1,068)	(1,183)
Net fixed assets	533	901	1,032	917
Other assets[7]	44	52	55	55
Total assets	**$2,563**	**$4,012**	**$5,892**	**$4,078**
Line of credit—bank[8]	194	773	1,436	-0-
Trade accounts payable[9]	560	888	1,619	833
Accrued expenses[10]	45	66	97	101
Bank debt, current portion[11]	55	102	118	102
Current liabilities[12]	**854**	**1,829**	**3,270**	**1,036**
Long-term bank debt[13]	423	683	947	825
Shareholder debt[14]	-0-	100	150	150
Total liabilities[15]	**1,277**	**2,612**	**4,367**	**2,011**
Owner's equity[16]	**1,286**	**1,400**	**1,525**	**2,067**
Total liabilities and equity[17]	**$2,563**	**$4,012**	**$5,892**	**$4,078**

Notes:

1. Plugged at $100.
2. Forecast at thirty-five receivable days.
3. Forecast at fifty-eight inventory days.
4. Forecast at 0.8 percent of revenue.
5. Determined by capital expenditure plans.
6. Obtained from depreciation schedule from the CPA.
7. Determined by knowledge of what is contained in this account.
8. A balancing number if needed. It is the last number to be determined by the workbook in the balance sheet forecast. In this case, zero indicating that a line of credit balance will not be necessary.
9. Forecast at thirty-two payable days.
10. Forecast at 0.7 percent of revenue.
11. Obtained from loan schedule from the CPA.
12. Determined by subtracting long-term liabilities from total liabilities.
13. Obtained from loan schedule from the CPA.
14. Held over from the prior year, per bank requirements.
15. Determined by subtracting equity from total liabilities and equity.
16. Equity is determined by adding forecast net profit to the prior year's equity, less a distribution to the owner of $317 (with the permission of the bank).
17. Plugged by the workbook as equal to total assets.

SUMMARY

Forecasting the balance sheet is fairly straightforward. All you need to do is make a few assumptions, based on questions like:

1. What is the minimum cash that you want on hand at the end of the year?
2. What is the desired receivable days?
3. What is the desirable inventory days?
4. What is the historical average of other current assets as a percentage of revenue?
5. What capital expenditures do you expect to make in the coming year?
6. What is the desirable payable days?
7. What is the average of accrued expenses, and other current liabilities as a percentage of revenue?
8. How much of the forecasted net profit do you expect to distribute to owners or pay in income tax?

It is neither necessary nor realistic to forecast the balance sheet to the nearest dollar. This exercise is intended to come up with a reasonable approximation of what the balance sheet will look like at the end of the year, and you should feel free to round off at least to the nearest thousand, or even more depending on the size of your business.

Do not get lost in all the numbers and do not do any of these calculations by hand. *Business Mastery*, an Excel-based workbook, is available to assist you in your forecasting efforts. Download it from www.60minutecfo.com

It is a simple matter of arithmetic to calculate the ratios and cash flow Once you have forecasted the income statement and balance sheet.

These forecasts are discussed in the next chapter.

Keep it simple and keep on paddling!

CHAPTER TEN: FORECASTING CASH FLOW & OPERATING PERFORMANCE

10

INTRODUCTION

It's great to know what your cash flow *has been*. Thanks to **Business Mastery**, it is now easy to forecast *what your cash flow is going to be.* Cash is King, and being able to forecast it is very useful, especially when communicating with your banker.

FORECASTED CASH FLOW

OPERATING CASH FLOW

Net profit	$859
Change in current assets less cash	1,695
Change in current liabilities less bank/shareholder debt	(782)
Change in net fixed assets	115
Change in non-current assets	(0)
Equals operating cash flow	**$1,887**

$1,887 ÷ $14,400 = 13.1% = **Oper. cash flow margin (OpCFM)**

FINANCING CASH FLOW

Change in bank debt	($1,574)
Change in shareholder debt	-0-
Change in other long-term debt	-0-
Equity adjustment	(317)
Equals financing cash flow	**($1,891)**

($1,891) ÷ $14,400 = (13.1%) = **Fin. cash flow margin (FinCFM)**

Net Cash Flow

Operating cash flow	$1,887
Financing cash flow	(1,891)
Equals net cash flow	**($4)**

($4) ÷ $14,400 = 0.03% = **Net cash flow margin (NetCFM)**

The financial ratios and cash flow margins forecast for 20X7 are on the following page.

Durson Distributors
Ratio Forecasts

	20X4	20X5	20X6	Planned 20X7	Industry Average
Liquidity					
Current ratio	2.33	1.67	1.47	**3.00**	1.60
Safety					
Debt-to-equity	0.99	1.87	2.86	**0.97**	1.70
Survival score	6.1	4.1	3.3	**6.9**	5.0
Profitability					
Gross profit margin	34.8%	34.1%	33.4%	**34.0%**	34.1%
Operating profit margin	3.6%	3.6%	3.0%	**6.6%**	5.5%
Net profit margin	2.6%	2.0%	1.4%	**6.0%**	4.7%
Operating Performance					
Return on equity (ROE)	13.1%	13.3%	12.4%	**41.5%**	31.3%
Receivable days	47 days	53 days	56 days	**35 days**	37 days
Inventory days	84 days	94 days	109 days	**58 days**	60 days
Payable days	48 days	54 days	68 days	**32 days**	41 days
Rev. per admin employee	$252.1	$241.5	$229.8	**$252.6**	$300.0
Cash Flow					
Operating cash flow margin	(11.1%)	(10.2%)	(7.0%)	**13.1%**	NA
Financing cash flow margin	7.9%	10.0%	7.1%	**(13.1%)**	NA
Net cash flow margin	(3.2%)	(0.2%)	0.1%	**(0.0%)**	NA

The news for 20X7 is easy to see, and it is all good.

1. Liquidity, as reflected by the current ratio, has improved substantially and is now above the industry average.

2. Safety, as reflected by the debt-to-equity ratio, has improved substantially and is now better than the industry average.

3. Profit margins have all improved substantially, and the operating and net profit margins are both above the industry averages.

4. Return on equity has improved and is now well above the industry average.

5. Receivable days were forecasted at thirty-five days, and this will be achieved by dedicating a person to calling all the delinquent accounts.

6. Inventory days were forecasted at fifty-eight days, and this will be accomplished by monitoring inventory turnover regularly.

7. Payable days were forecasted at thirty-two days and forecasted liquidity and operating cash flow is sufficient to produce this result.

8. The Survival score has improved to above the 20X4 level and exceeds the excellent standard of 5.0.

9. Operating cash flow is a positive $1,887 thanks to higher turnover of accounts receivable and inventory. As assets go *down*, cash flow goes *up*.

10. Strong operating cash flow allowed for a significant reduction in bank and trade debt.

11. Revenue per admin employee improved and is closer to the goal of $300.

This analysis is not complicated. It is obvious. Give it 60 minutes a month, and one step at a time, you will know it cold. That's a promise.

SUMMARY OF THE 20X7 PLANNING PROCESS.

Durson Distributors was in financial trouble at the end of 20X6 and on the verge of losing their bank financing. Allen Durson grew the company at a rapid rate and used existing cash, bank debt, trade debt, and shareholder debt to finance this growth. Operating cash flow was negative for all three years of his leadership, and there was no one in the company who had any idea that a serious financial problem was developing until it was almost too late.

Allen's focus was on revenue. Everyone was working hard, and things like accounts receivable collection and expense control were neglected. This pattern is what happens when a company grows rapidly, and no one is monitoring a few key ratios. I have seen this happen many times, and it is avoidable if the principles in this book are employed, and growth is carefully managed. *No one* can grow as fast as they want because all firms are constrained by available equity and cash flow.

This case study illustrates that:
1. excess growth can be undesirable
2. that you cannot determine the financial condition of your business by just looking at the *numbers* on your financial statements. You must also look at key *relationships*.
3. You need to know what relationships to look at and why you are looking at them for this to be possible.
4. Profits do not equal cash flow, so do not ever assume that the more you make, the more cash you will have.

Julian may have comfortable in the plunder phase of business, but Allen knew that growth was necessary and took the company into the blunder phase and near insolvency. It took only one year of more moderate growth to move the company into the thunder phase. The goal going forward is to stay there.

Establishing your business plan provides a blueprint for what you expect to happen and allows you to correct any financial problems that you might have. This plan is powerful information that less than 1 or 2 percent of all business owners ever have.

Pledge to yourself that you will never end up like Durson in 20X3 or 20X6. Your goal should be to get to the thunder phase of business *and stay there*. Easier said than done, but with careful planning and management of your financial relationships and by applying the principles contained in this book, you can make this happen.

Keep this book on your credenza and refer to it regularly. Use it or lose it.

20X8—ONE YEAR LATER

At the beginning of 20X7, Allen sat down with his leadership team and designed a profit-sharing program based upon sharing any profit over a threshold based on a return on assets (net profit ÷ total assets). A consultant told them that a good return on assets to use for their industry is 10 percent, and that is what they chose as a minimum return for the company.

A base net profit was set at $589 (10 percent x total assets of $5,892). They decided to share 50 percent of any profit over $589, which would be shared equally by all employees. They explained this profit-sharing program to the employees and then informed them monthly how the company was doing.

When the employees realized that they could make a bonus if the company exceeded the $589 net profit level, they began to focus on how they could help the company become more profitable. In other words, they began to think like owners.

At the end of 20X7, the company had an actual net profit of $965,000 (exceeding the forecast amount of $859,000), and $188,000 went into the profit-sharing pool ($965,000 - $589,000 x .5). As a result, each of the 62 employees received a check for $3000. This bonus was a meaningful amount of money, and the employees were overwhelmed. Some were tearful when they received their check.

The company won, the employees won, the Durson family won, the trade creditors won, and the bank won. It was a happy holiday party, and the future looked bright.

The type of profit-sharing plan described above has the advantage of motivating the employees to think like owners. They become highly focused on building the profitability of the company because they understand that they will share in any profits more than the threshold. They appreciate being able to share in the amount that exceeds the minimum goal. If you do not currently have a formal bonus or profit-sharing program, this is one that you might consider. I have seen it work very well with many clients.

SUMMARY

Think about the power of understanding the financial performance of your business on a historical basis. Discovering where you have been and your financial strengths and weaknesses. Determining what you need to do to improve.

Think about the power of going through the planning and forecasting exercise and having your key management involved and committed to achieving the plan.

Think about the power of presenting your historical analysis and financial forecasts to your banker. Probably less than 5 percent of the bank's customers ever prepare this type of information.

Your banker will be impressed and feel confident that you know and understand what you are doing from a financial standpoint. Your bank relations will be strengthened, and you will most likely get what you ask for in the way of bank loans *because you won't ask for something you don't deserve.*

Pledge to start preparing a financial plan if you are not already doing so. Don't worry about the details of the entire process—simply get started. Follow the general guidelines as outlined in this book. Get help from your banker, CPA, and other financial advisors. The important thing is to get started and make this a routine part of your managing process.

HOMEWORK ASSIGNMENT

Layout a planning timetable for your business, starting in the fall and finishing soon after the end of the year (assuming you are on a December 31 fiscal year). Consult with your leadership team to determine the attendees, content, and format of your planning meetings. Make sure your sales team is engaged in the process.

Download a copy of *Business Mastery*, an Excel-based workbook, from www.60minutecfo.com, and make a forecast for the current year. Set realistic goals for your company and determine what your cash flow and ratios will look like at the end of the year.

What happened to Durson from 20X4 to 20X6 is typical of companies that are driven by growth, and it is illustrative of how quickly you can get into serious trouble without an understanding of the financial dynamics of your company. It is also illustrative of how quickly things can be turned around once you understand the basics and adhere to the principles outlined in this book.

Use *Business Mastery* to calculate the financial ratios discussed in this book monthly. Re-read chapters one through four in this book. Know and understand these ratios so well that you don't have to think about what they mean. Make sure your leadership team knows and understands them as well.

We have looked at some relationships to determine the health of your business and any areas that might need improvement. We have used that information to forecast the future, something that less than 5 percent of all businesses do. Congratulations on paddling this far!

The rest of this book is devoted to additional topics that will enhance your survival and operating success. Use *Business Mastery* and give this analysis 60 minutes a month. In a very short period, you and your leadership team will gain a clear understanding of business finance. This exercise is neither difficult nor complicated, but it is unlikely to occur without constant repetition.

The next chapter will discuss how to calculate break-even revenue.

Keep it simple, and keep on paddling!

CHAPTER ELEVEN: CALCULATING BREAK-EVEN REVENUE

11

INTRODUCTION

In chapter two we discussed the importance of separating expenses into two types, direct and indirect. This classification allows you to determine your gross profit (revenue minus direct expenses) and gross profit margin (gross profit divided by revenue). The gross profit margin is one of the most important ratios that you calculate.

In this chapter, we separate expenses by how they *behave, fixed* or *variable*. This classification is useful because knowing how your expenses behave will allow you to calculate your revenue break-even level and help you to determine the optimal operation leverage (mix of fixed and variable expenses) for your business.

You should calculate your break-even revenue, both annually and monthly. If revenue declines, you will know how far it can fall before you begin to lose money, and you will know how much you need to cut in fixed expenses to avoid a loss.

EXPENSE BEHAVIOR PATTERNS

FIXED EXPENSES
Fixed expenses are those that do not go up or down with revenue. Examples include rent, depreciation, insurance, administrative salaries, and utilities. They do not vary on an incremental basis with revenue.

VARIABLE EXPENSES
Variable expenses are caused by revenue and tend to go up or down with revenue. Examples include direct wages, inventory expense, bad debts, and sales commissions.

All your direct expenses are not variable, and all your indirect expenses are not fixed. If you are not sure whether an expense is fixed or variable, always classify it as fixed. The higher fixed expense will give you a higher break-even revenue level and therefore be a more conservative estimate of your break-even revenue.

BOTH FIXED AND VARIABLE
Some expenses, such as vehicle operating expenses, contain both fixed (depreciation insurance, and license) and variable (fuel, tires, repairs) components. Depreciation, title, and insurance should be classified as a

fixed expense, and the balance of vehicle operating expenses can be classified as variable.

OPERATIONAL LEVERAGE

The relationship between fixed and variable expenses is referred to as "operational leverage." High fixed expenses and low variable expenses produce a higher break-even revenue level and, therefore a higher risk of loss.

High operational leverage (high fixed and low variable expenses) produces higher business risk in the same manner as does high financial leverage (high debt-to-equity ratio as discussed in chapter one). High financial leverage, when combined with high operational leverage, significantly increases the overall risk of the business.

You can reduce the amount of operational leverage by changing some expenses from fixed to variable. One example would be to pay your salespeople a commission rather than a salary.

HIGH FIXED EXPENSES, LOW VARIABLE EXPENSES

High fixed expenses increase your break-even revenue level, your potential profit, and potential loss: high risk and high reward. If you combine high financial risk with high operational risk, the level of the overall risk of the company is increased significantly.

LOW FIXED EXPENSES, HIGH VARIABLE EXPENSES

Low fixed expenses reduce your break-even revenue level but also reduce the potential profit and the potential loss. Diagrams illustrating high fixed versus low fixed expense are on the following page.

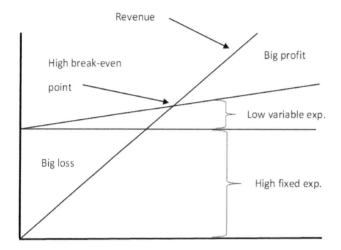

Large potential profit and large potential loss. Higher break-even point. More risk, more reward.

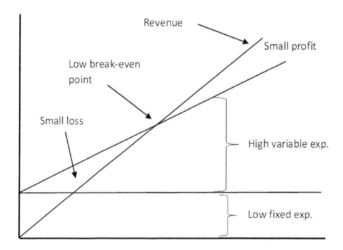

Small potential profit and small potential loss. Lower break-even point. Less risk, less reward

When you convert a fixed expense, like sales salary, to a variable expense, like sales commission, you have reduced your break-even revenue level and you have reduced your potential profit. If your business is both cyclical and seasonal, you might opt to convert fixed expenses to variable whenever possible. Study the operational leverage options, and then strategize what will work best for your company.

Calculate your monthly break-even revenue and work to develop a business strategy that will meet or exceed that level every month.

FOUR STEPS TO DETERMINE BREAK-EVEN REVENUE

You determine the break-even revenue level by the following four steps:

1. Separate expenses into fixed and variable.
2. Subtract variable expenses from revenue to determine the contribution margin.
3. Divide the contribution margin by revenue to get the contribution margin ratio (CMR).
4. Divide fixed expenses by the contribution margin ratio (CMR) to calculate break-even revenue.

STEP ONE: SEPARATE EXPENSES INTO FIXED AND VARIABLE

The following is a typical breakdown of fixed and variable expenses.

Fixed Expenses	Variable Expenses
Depreciation	Direct wages
Rent	Commissions
Advertising	Vehicle operating expenses[1]
Office expense	Supplies
Insurance	Bad debts
Legal and accounting	Other direct expense
Other administrative expense	
Administrative salaries	
Business taxes and licenses	
Payroll tax and benefits[2]	
Repairs and maintenance	
Telephone and utilities	
Travel and entertainment	
Other income[3]	
Other expense	
Interest[4]	

1. Some elements of vehicle operating expense are fixed, such as depreciation, license, and insurance.
2. Payroll taxes and benefits associated with direct wages are variable.
3. Other income is not an expense but is added here as a deduction to Other Expense.
4. Interest on bank debt is always included in fixed expenses.

STEP TWO: DETERMINE THE CONTRIBUTION MARGIN

We determine the contribution margin by subtracting variable expenses from revenue, as follows:

Revenue minus variable expenses equal **Contribution margin**

STEP THREE: CALCULATE THE CONTRIBUTION MARGIN RATIO (CMR)

We calculate the contribution margin ratio by dividing the contribution margin by revenue, as follows:

$$\frac{\text{Contribution Margin}}{\text{Revenue}} = \text{Contribution Margin Ratio (CMR)}$$

STEP FOUR: DIVIDE FIXED EXPENSES BY THE CMR

$$\frac{\text{Fixed expenses}}{\text{Contribution margin ratio}} = \text{Break-even revenue}$$

CASE STUDY: DURSON DISTRIBUTORS

STEP ONE: SEPARATE EXPENSES INTO FIXED AND VARIABLE

	20X6	Fixed	Variable
Revenue	$13,100		
Cost of goods sold			8,725
Advertising		180	
Bad debts			95
Depreciation		126	
Equipment Leases		88	
Insurance		201	
Legal and accounting		33	
Other administrative expense		81	
Office expense		71	
Payroll tax and benefits		412	
Rent		325	
Repairs & Maintenance		31	
Admin salaries		1,480	
Sales commissions			393
Business tax and license		72	
Telephone & utilities		52	
Travel & entertainment		147	
Vehicle Expense		201	
Other income		(28)	
Other expense		51	
Interest expense		175	
Total		3,698	9,213

STEP TWO: DETERMINE THE CONTRIBUTION MARGIN

Revenue	$13,100
Variable expenses	(9,213)
Contribution margin	**$3,887**

STEP THREE: CALCULATE THE CONTRIBUTION MARGIN RATIO (CMR)

$$\frac{3,887}{13,100} = \mathbf{29.7\%}$$

STEP FOUR: DIVIDE FIXED EXPENSES BY THE CONTRIBUTION MARGIN RATIO (CMR)

$$\frac{3,698}{.297} = \mathbf{\$12,463} \qquad \textbf{Break-even revenue}$$

Monthly break-even revenue is calculated by dividing annual break-even revenue by twelve:

$$\$12,463 \div 12 = \$1,039 \qquad \textbf{monthly break-even revenue}$$

Allen has now learned some important aspects of the business that can help him plan for increased profitability. One is that he can now determine what revenue level is required to obtain the desired profit. To produce a return on equity of 30 percent, net profit needs to be $458 (.30 x equity of $1,525).

Calculate the revenue needed to achieve that profit using the following formula:

$$\frac{\text{Fixed expenses} + \text{desired profit}}{\text{Contribution margin ratio}} = \textbf{Required revenue}$$

$$\frac{3{,}698 + 458}{.297} = \begin{array}{l}\textbf{Required} \quad \textbf{revenue} \quad \textbf{of} \\ \textbf{\$14,007}\end{array}$$

If Durson's rent is going up $50k in 20X7, Allen can calculate the revenue he needs to make a profit of $458 plus $50 in increased fixed expense by adding $50 to fixed expense as follows:

$$\frac{3{,}698 + 458 + 50}{.297} = \begin{array}{l}\textbf{Required} \quad \textbf{revenue} \quad \textbf{of} \\ \textbf{\$14,175}\end{array}$$

Knowing how your expenses *behave*, either on a fixed or variable basis, allows you to calculate revenue needed to either break even or generate a specific net profit. Break-even analysis is a valuable exercise to assist you in financial planning.

STRATEGY FOR CORRECTING A LOSS

Let's assume that Duson Distributors experienced below break-even revenue as follows:

Revenue	$11,253
Variable expenses[1]	(7,911)
Contribution margin	3,342
Fixed expenses	(3,698)
Net profit	(356)

[1] Calculated by multiplying the revenue of $11,253 by 100% minus 29.7% or 70.3%.

The only way to correct this loss is to either increase revenue to the break-even level ($12,463) or cut fixed expenses by $356. Fixed expenses are the ones to cut, since cutting variable expenses would necessitate cutting revenue (variable expenses are caused by and directly related to revenue). The only way to do this is to determine your fixed and variable expenses, then target the fixed expenses that should be cut.

This expense behavior analysis is valuable and informative. If we had not gone through this exercise for Durson Distributors, we would not know exactly how to correct the above loss situation example. Since we did, we know that Allen must look carefully at his *fixed* expenses to see which ones can be reduced. He should act promptly and do this as soon as the loss is experienced, as discussed in chapter sixteen.

SUMMARY

Break-even revenue is a study of how expenses behave (fixed or variable) versus their type (direct or indirect). High fixed expenses produce a high break-even revenue and a large potential profit, while high variable expenses produce a low break-even level and a smaller potential profit. High fixed expenses; high reward and high risk. High variable expenses; low reward and low risk. You should strategize which expenses you can convert from fixed to variable and vice versa to determine the optimal amount of operational leverage for your firm. Calculating the monthly break-even will let you know what revenue is required to at least break-even or make a profit every month. High-profit firms make it a point to diversify, if possible so that they are profitable every month.

Do not worry about the formulas in this chapter, and do not calculate your break-even revenue by hand. Download the *Business Break-even* workbook from www.60minutecfo.com and use it to calculate the break-even revenue for your business, both annually and monthly.

The next chapter will discuss capital budgeting and how to analyze equipment purchases.

Keep it simple, and keep on paddling!

CHAPTER TWELVE: CAPITAL BUDGETING

INTRODUCTION

The capital budgeting exercise discussed in this chapter can help you to determine whether it is financially wise to purchase a fixed asset. This analysis is especially valuable for an equipment-intensive business. ○

Despite the benefits of using this tool, virtually no business uses a capital expenditure analysis. The reasons are primarily because most business owners think about this simplistically. They ask and answer two questions; "Do I need the equipment?" and "Can I afford it?" If the answer is yes to both questions, the analysis is over.

Decisions to buy fixed assets are based upon experience and gut instincts, and most of the time, they are probably correct. There is a tool outlined in this chapter. However, that can augment gut feelings with a little more formal analysis and perhaps avoid a costly mistake. Capital expenditures represent a significant amount of the company's financial resources and are a multi-year decision, so it is prudent to do this analysis to make sure that it is a sound financial decision.

DEFINITION

Capital budgeting is defined as *the practice of allocating funds for investment in fixed assets in the most effective manner*. It is the process of determining whether an asset should be purchased based upon its forecasted cash flows.

EXAMPLE

Your delivery van is getting on in years, and the transmission goes out. Should you repair it or buy a new one? Capital budgeting is the answer to this and all other questions regarding the purchase of fixed assets, and this chapter describes the process that you should use.

STEPS IN THE CAPITAL BUDGETING PROCESS

1. Estimate the annual net cash income
2. Estimate salvage value
3. Establish an acceptable return on the asset

STEP ONE - ESTIMATE THE ANNUAL NET CASH INCOME.

Estimate the net cash income (cash inflow minus cash outflow) each year for five years that will be generated by the equipment. Do not include depreciation, which is a non-cash expense, in this process, but you can add the income tax savings of the depreciation into the cash income.

Net cash income either estimated as a level amount over five years, or it may vary from year to year. Of course, it may be difficult to look out for five years, but this is not intended to be an exact science. Your best guess is sufficient, and it is wise to be conservative. If you have no idea how much a vehicle or piece of equipment will generate in net cash income for your business over five years, then it is questionable that you should purchase it in the first place. The only reason to do purchase equipment is to generate income (or reduce expense if it is a replacement for existing equipment), and you should at least try to determine how much that might be.

Note in this exercise that a reduction in expenses (labor, repairs, etc.) that will occur as the result of buying an asset has the same impact as an increase in income in determining the net cash flow.

STEP TWO - ESTIMATE THE SALVAGE VALUE.

Estimate the salvage value of the equipment at the end of five years and add that to the fifth-year cash income. Salvage value can either be determined by using a percentage of the initial cost of the equipment (like 10% of the initial cost), or you can use historical experience in buying and selling the equipment. Many items of used equipment have an established market value, and the value for a five-year-old truck can be compared to the original purchase price. Estimating zero salvage value, especially for assets like computers, would be the most conservative approach.

STEP THREE - ESTABLISH A RATE OF RETURN.

Establish a minimum acceptable rate of return required on the purchased asset. Fifteen percent should be a minimum for any industry, and a higher rate would be appropriate if the future profitability of the equipment is somewhat uncertain.

For this exercise, always assume that you are paying cash for the equipment even if you expect to finance it with a long-term loan. The present value of the cash outflow is the initial cost of the equipment, plus shipping and setup, if required, less any cash received for an item you are replacing.

Do not worry about any formulas in this chapter, and do not do any calculations by hand. *Business Equipment*, an Excel workbook that comes with this book. Download it at www.60MinuteCFO.com

CASE STUDY: DURSON DISTRIBUTORS

The business has grown, and there is a need for an additional delivery van. A used truck was located that is available for $40,000.

STEP ONE:

Allen estimates that the truck will generate $11,000 in net cash income (cash income minus cash expense) per year. (This amount is illustrative for purposes of this example and is not intended to reflect what a truck might generate in your business.)

STEP TWO:

Salvage value is estimated to be $7,000 at the end of five years.

STEP THREE:

Allen has decided that a minimum rate of return is 15%.

Calculations

Year	Net Cash Flow		Present Value Factor	=	Present Value
0	($40,000)	x	1.0	=	($40,000)
1	$11,000	x	0.870	=	$9,570
2	$11,000	x	0.756	=	$8,316
3	$11,000	x	0.658	=	$7,238
4	$11,000	x	0.572	=	$6,292
5	$18,000[1]	x	0.497	=	$8,946
Net present value[2]					$362

[1].$11,000 plus $7,000 salvage value.

[2]. The present value of the cash inflow minus the present value of the cash outflow.

The present value factors used in this example are for a 15 percent return on investment. We know that the return on this truck is more than 15 percent because the net present value is a positive $362. If the net present value were zero, we would know that the return is *exactly* 15 percent, and if the net present value were negative, we would know that the return is *less* than 15 percent.

If the net present value is negative, the investment should be rejected since it does not produce the required minimum return on investment.

Present value factors for various returns:

year	15%	20%	25%	30%
0	1.0	1.0	1.0	1.0
1	0.870	0.833	0.800	0.769
2	0.756	0.694	0.640	0.592
3	0.658	0.579	0.512	0.455
4	0.572	0.482	0.410	0.350
5	0.497	0.402	0.328	0.269

SUMMARY

Acquisition of fixed assets requires committing a large portion of your company's resources over an extended number of years, and these types of decisions, therefore, deserve to be analyzed as carefully as possible. If your company has six potential capital investments in the coming year, and only enough financial resources to fund five of them, calculate the estimated net present value of all six and pick the five highest.

The most difficult part of this exercise is certainly not the actual calculations. Those are simple arithmetic, and *Business Equipment* is available with this book to do it for you. Download it at www.60minutecfo.com. The challenging aspect of the exercise is forecasting the cash returns for five years with any degree of certainty, but if you have no idea how much a piece of equipment might generate in income, *you should not buy it.* Purchasing a fixed asset is an important economic decision that should not be based on gut instincts.

Go through this exercise even if you are not completely sure how or why it works. Give it your best shot. This analysis is better than nothing, and you will gain greater understanding each time you use it. Do not do any of these calculations by hand. Download the *Business Equipment* workbook from www.60minutecfo.com.

The next chapter will discuss how to always get what you ask for at the bank.

Keep it simple, and keep on paddling!

CHAPTER THIRTEEN: TAKE IT TO THE BANK

13

INTRODUCTION

Business owners have a difficult time understanding bankers and how they make their decisions, which often appear to be arbitrary. Because of this they are cautious in what they disclose beyond the requested financial statements. This gap in communications prohibits the formation of a relationship that is essential to the success of both parties.

An understanding of the financial analysis principles discussed in chapters one through four and the planning procedures outlined in chapters seven through ten ensure that the busienss owner and the banker will be on the same page and communicating effectively. It is all about being prepared before stepping foot inside the bank.

Financial terms are understood and communication with the banker is no longer a mystery. Bankers seek to learn what is clearly revealed in the *Move Mastery* workbook, and business owners gain the ability to anticipate and answer questions before they are asked. They understand that disclosing *more* rather than *less* information is in their best interests, and helps to establish trust.

The business owner and the banker need to be on the same team, pulling in the same harness in the same direction. Understanding and trust enables this to happen. Customers who come into the bank with all of the analysis completed and financial forecasts for the year ahead are unheard of, and welcomed with enthusiasm.

In chapter six we saw that Allen grew Durson Movers very quickly, wound up with hugely negative operating cash flow, increased borrowing, and a substantially higher debt-to-equity ratio. Like most business owners, Allen was revenue-driven and had no understanding of why the bank was upset about this decline in safety. He was working hard, making great progress and things were developing exactly as he had hoped.

Prior to this experience he believed that the only thing that stood in the way of Durson Movers being a very successful company was access to an unlimited supply of loans. He learned the hard way that business owners need to be aware of and measure the financial condition of their company on a regular basis. This analysis isn't difficult, but it wasn't done.

The key to getting what you ask for at the bank is to supply the information that they are going to require at the outset. Prior preparation is essential. Information should be supplied, such as:

1. What is the financial condition of your business, both current and the trend over previous years?
2. Where do you visualize your business going in the next year?
3. How do you plan to get there?
4. What is your forecasted cash flow?
5. What are your anticipated borrowing requirements, both for fixed asset purchases and line of credit?
6. Does your financial condition and forecast support your ability to pay the proposed bank debt?
7. How will loans be repaid if your forecasts are overly optimistic and the repayment plan is jeopardized?

In seeking this information, your banker is doing their job and protecting you in the process. A good banker is not going to grant you a loan that you may have difficulty repaying, even if it is 100 percent collateralized. The bank is there to help you be successful not loan you into trouble, and the bank does not want to have to deal with your collateral if the loan is not repaid.

GOOD COMMUNICATIONS

Being well prepared and able to answer the above questions will take your relationship to new heights, ensure that your banker becomes an integral member of your team, and that you get what you need from the bank to successfully finance your business. You and your banker will be on the same page, communicating effectively about the financial condition and future direction of your business. Good communication about the financial condition of your business is paramount in establishing a successful relationship with your banker and understanding the principles of financial management that are described in this book are the keys to good communication.

When you complete your historical analysis and financial forecasts, you gain significant credibility as someone who has a grasp of your business from a financial standpoint. You will rise to the top 1 or 2 percent of the bank's customers who provide such information. You and your banker will be working in harmony for the financial success of your business.

Granting loans is how the bank makes money, and it is always looking to make loans to good, profitable, well-run businesses. Your business will be in that category after learning and applying the principles of this book.

STRUCTURING DEBT VS. EQUITY

The two sources that are available to provide funds for your business are debt (money from banks, finance companies, trade creditors, and other lenders), and equity (money from owners). The rule for financing a business is *equity first, debt second*. A strong equity base allows you to work from a position of strength when you seek debt. With a low debt-to-equity ratio, you will be less risky, and debt will, therefore, be less expensive (in the form of lower interest rates). Your debt-to-equity ratio is likely to be high in the wonder and blunder phases of business, and it will, therefore, be more difficult and expensive to obtain bank financing.

The reverse is also true. If you seek debt first and reach or exceed your borrowing limits and then seek equity capital out of desperation, you will have to give up much more in the way of ownership to raise the needed capital. Your company will be risky, and equity capital will be both difficult and expensive to obtain.

EQUITY FINANCING

Equity first, debt second. It sounds simple enough, but it may not always be possible. Where will you get equity capital? A full discussion of angel financing, venture capital, or public offerings is beyond the scope of this book; however, only a small minority of start-up or existing businesses will qualify for any of that. You are most likely limited to either raising money yourself (available savings, sale or mortgage of your home, etc.) or hitting up the four Fs, founders, friends, family and fools.

If you have already put all your available funds into the business, then your options are limited to friends and family. In fact, your options are limited to *older* friends and family who have lived long enough to accumulate the money needed to help you. Putting money in your business, however, may not be exactly where they ought to invest funds set aside for retirement.

You should think very carefully about borrowing from friends or family. Initial business plans are based upon supreme optimism and are seldom achieved. If loans are not repaid there is a strong likelihood that relationships may be damaged, perhaps irreparably. You should think about whether borrowing to start a business is worth that risk. Fully documented agreements will help in reducing subsequent legal arguments.

While equity financing may be tough, a minimum amount needs to be provided to ensure continued financial viability. Financial forecasts, as discussed in chapters eight through ten, can indicate how much capital will likely be required. Update the forecasts frequently, as information regarding actual performance is available. Remember the rule of thumb that it always takes twice as long to grow revenue, and twice as much capital as initially planned.

If you intend to raise equity capital from the general public, seek the advice of qualified lawyers, accountants, and business valuation experts who are experienced in this type of transaction. The legal requirements are complicated, and this is *not* a do-it-yourself project. Prepare a detailed business and financial plan, be aware of liabilities to which you may be exposed and make sure you get proper legal assistance.

DEBT FINANCING

The discussion concerning debt financing in the rest of this chapter will assume that a commercial bank is the source of the funds. The general principles also apply to other sources of debt, such as business factors, finance or leasing companies, savings and loans, insurance companies, credit unions, and the government.

If traditional bank financing is not available to you, research other publications for more detailed information. The Small Business Association has an extensive list of publications that can provide information about financing sources and available programs. Also be sure to seek the advice and counsel of SCORE mentors. Call the local SCORE office for this free assistance.

STRUCTURING DEBT

Depending upon the phase of business (refer to the Introduction) most businesses require three categories of debt.

1. Short-term debt (a line of credit due in less than one year)
2. Intermediate-term debt (short-term debt extends beyond 12 months)
3. Long-term debt (due in more than one year)

All your loans will fall into one of these categories, and it's important that you understand the type of debt you need from the bank. This involves answering the following questions:

1. How much are you going to need?
2. How long will you need it?
3. How do you expect to pay it back?

You'd be amazed at the number of business owners who cannot answer these questions with any degree of accuracy or sophistication when they request a loan from a bank. They rely instead on instincts and a seat-of-the-pants approach to financing their business. Then, when they do not get a warm reception at the bank, they complain that bankers are not there to help. Getting what you need at the bank requires answering these questions and a knowledge of basic finance as outlined in this book.

SHORT-TERM DEBT

Short-term bank debt is due within one year. It can take the form of a fixed maturity loan, such as 90 or 120 days, or it can be structured in the form of a line of credit that is negotiated at the beginning of the year and made available as needed. It is used to finance seasonal cash flow needs, such as an increase in accounts receivable during a peak season. Interest is usually floating, but it might be set for the year. The expectation is that the line of credit will start at zero at the beginning of the year, rise to some predicted level during the peak season, and fall to zero at or before the end of the fiscal year.

Collateral for a line of credit is usually accounts receivables, and banks will generally provide up to 75 percent of your accounts receivable less than ninety days old. This is good motivation ensure that you manage your receivable days (refer to chapter three).

INTERMEDIATE-TERM DEBT

The need for intermediate-term bank debt occurs when some of your line of credit remains unpaid at the end of the year. Bankers usually tolerate this initially, but not on a regular basis. It is an indication that your working capital and operating cash flow are not adequate to fund your business. The goal is to pay off your line of credit by the end of the year and not have any intermediate-term bank debt. The forecasting in Move Mastery will help determine how and when this will be achieved.

Be sure to communicate your plans and forecasts with your banker so that they are informed.

LONG-TERM DEBT

Long-term debt is used for the purchase of fixed assets. The amount of the loan is limited to a percentage of the cost or value of the asset. The term is usually three to five years, depending on the asset. Land and buildings can typically be financed for up to twenty years, but it's not a good idea from a tax standpoint to own real estate assets inside your company (talk to your CPA to understand why this is the case). Regular monthly payments are required, and interest can be either fixed or floating. Collateral consists of the asset purchased, and sometimes all the other equipment as well.

Even though it is straightforward, banks are sometimes less eager to make long-term loans. The reason is that the banker must determine your ability to make payments several years into the future, and this presents more uncertainty and therefore more risk. The equipment is available for collateral, but the bank is not in the equipment sales business and does not relish going through this process. For this reason, long-term loans are usually only available to well-established businesses that have a good payment record and a demonstrated track record of profitability.

Leasing fixed assets is an alternative to buying, and sometimes the credit requirements are less strict for this type of transaction. Ask your CPA for help and advice on leasing equipment, since structuring a lease is a complex exercise from a tax standpoint.

LOAN AGREEMENT

Most loans are covered by a loan agreement, and you can expect to negotiate loan covenants as part of this agreement. Covenants may take the form of a minimum current ratio, a maximum debt-to-equity ratio, a minimum interest coverage ratio, or a minimum dollar amount of working capital or equity. There also may be restrictions on owner's compensation, dividends, and repayment of shareholder loans.

These covenants are negotiable, and you should be cautious about agreeing to any that you are not confident you can achieve. Failure to comply with any of the loan covenants allows the bank to demand immediate repayment of the loan balance. The bank may temporarily waive the covenant, but you don't want to count on this. Some of the covenants may be confusing or unfamiliar. If you do not understand any of the covenants proposed by the bank, be sure to keep asking until you do.

You should also be cautious about tying up all your assets for a loan, thereby restricting your ability to finance your business in the future. Including accounts receivable as collateral for an equipment loan, as an example, makes it difficult or impossible to obtain a line of credit because your accounts receivable are securing other debt. Avoid this situation and agree to this only as a last resort.

INTEREST RATES

The factors that determine the interest rate that you will pay at the bank include:

1. The risk level of your business.
2. The cost of funds to the bank (interest on certificates of deposit, savings accounts, etc.).
3. The term of the loan (longer-term loans are usually riskier and therefore have a higher interest rate).
4. The amount of the loan (smaller loans cost as much to make as bigger loans and therefore may have a higher interest rate).
5. The collateral (some forms of collateral are more difficult to foreclose on and therefore costlier to administer).
6. The average balances that you maintain in your checking account (the more you maintain, the lower your rate).
7. The supply and demand for loanable funds.
8. The bank's competition.

All the above will determine your interest rate, but you should be aware that interest rates are often negotiable. Most lending officers have some discretion about the rates that they can charge, and you should inquire about this if you feel yours is too high.

If you determine that a competing bank is willing to offer the same type of loan at a lower interest rate, then go back to your bank with this information. The bank can either match the competition or risk losing your business. Don't be tempted to switch banks frequently to get a somewhat-lower interest rate. This tactic isn't likely to save you a lot of money, won't build loyalty between you and the bank, and may eventually hinder your ability to obtain bank loans.

THE FIVE C'S OF CREDIT

Bankers tend to look at a loan request within the context of the five Cs of credit. In order of importance, they are:

1. Character
2. Capacity
3. Capital
4. Collateral
5. Conditions

CHARACTER

Bankers want to look you in the eye and see an honest, ethical person. They do not want to work with people of marginal character, no matter how strong the deal. It is the most important criterion they have, and they will check you out as thoroughly as possible to see if your word is good.

CAPACITY

Once you pass the character test, you need to demonstrate that you have the capacity to repay the loan. This is done by establishing a track record and by presenting well-thought-out forecasts that indicate repayment is probable. *Business Mastery* will help in this process.

CAPITAL

Every business needs a sufficient base of capital (equity) to qualify for bank loans. The *amount* of required capital is a subjective judgment, but it will usually be tied to your debt-to-equity ratio, as discussed in chapter one. If your ratio is high, as it might be in the wonder or blunder phases of business, this will make obtaining bank loans more difficult, if not impossible. Before asking for a loan, put yourself in your banker's shoes, and ask yourself if you would loan money to a high-risk start-up business lacking a strong balance sheet and a track record of stable profitability.

COLLATERAL

There is an unwritten rule in banking that loans should not be granted solely based on available collateral because collateral does not make a bad loan good. It is still a bad loan. In other words, there should be every indication that the collateral will never be required and that it is only taken to allow the bank to recover its funds in the case of some unforeseen event. There are asset-based lenders who make loans based solely on collateral, but banks are not in this category.

Bankers always ask for collateral, and they always utilize accounts receivable, but it is only fourth in the order of importance as to whether they make a loan.

Strong, well-run, and financially stable businesses with good track records are able to borrow on an unsecured basis, but not many.

CONDITIONS

The last C refers to those conditions that are largely outside of your control—the economy, and the industry. Difficult economic times will negatively impact the willingness of banks to provide loans.

PERSONAL GUARANTEES

As you have probably experienced, bankers look for not one (cash flow), not two (collateral), but *three* sources of repayment. The third source is your personal guarantee.

For most business borrowers, bankers require the personal guarantees of the owners, but some businesses are strong enough to stand on their own and do not require the personal guarantee of the owner. If you feel that you are in this elite group, then speak up. Make your case. Let the banker tell you why you must personally guarantee the debt.

If you are making a loan request for the first time, state at the outset that you are not expecting to guarantee the loan. Test the waters. See what they say. In the final analysis, do not be reluctant to personally guarantee a loan. This position may indicate to the bank that you do not have confidence in the ability of the business to repay the loan. Personal liability is something that you want to avoid, but not at the expense of restricting your borrowing ability. In any case, it is perfectly OK to have this discussion with the bank if you feel the business should stand on its own.

RULES OF BEHAVIOR

There are a few rules of behavior that you should follow in building a good relationship with your banker.

RULE NUMBER ONE: ALWAYS BE PREPARED

Put yourself in your banker's place. What information would you want? What questions would you have? Anticipate these in advance and be prepared with answers. See Appendix III for an outline of how your bank proposal should be structured.

Fill out *Business Mastery* and discuss the strengths of your business from a financial standpoint and what you plan to do to work on the areas that need improvement. Compare your business to the RMA ratio averages for your business.

Educate your banker about your business and take the time to describe it thoroughly. Make sure you are proactive in mentioning any problems or weak areas that you have, describe what caused them, and what you plan to do about it.

Overkill with information. More is better. It will make a good first impression. You will be the first one in the history of the bank to come in with this analysis and they will be impressed!

RULE NUMBER TWO: WORK ON ESTABLISHING A GOOD RELATIONSHIP

Invite your banker to social functions, such as out on your boat (that you acquired in the thunder phase of business), to a football game, or the theater. Get to know them other on more than a business basis to deepen your relationship.

Understand that nothing will cement your relationship like getting your banker additional business. Refer prospective customers whenever possible.

Make sure your banker visits your business. Get your banker on your turf to meet your key people at least once a year.

Get to know your banker's boss, and maybe even the boss's boss. This ensures some degree of continuity when, or if, the lending officer handling your account changes.

If you are not hitting it off with the assigned lending officer, don't be bashful about requesting a replacement. It is important to have a good relationship with that person and the bank wants this as much as you do.

RULE NUMBER THREE—ALWAYS KEEP YOUR BANKER INFORMED

Provide accurate and timely information about your business. Send the bank quarterly financial statements, with appropriate comments and explanations.

You and perhaps your CFO or accounting manager should meet with the bank two to three times per year or more. Tell it all—the good and the bad. The bank will find out anyway and trying to hide or cover up something will hurt your credibility and your relationship.

Do not assume that all is well if you do not hear from the bank. Make a point to stay in touch and communicate regularly.

RULE NUMBER FOUR: NEVER SURPRISE YOUR BANKER
Bankers, like most people, do not like surprises.

There is a strong temptation to tell your bankers only what they want to hear. When they find out the rest of the story, they are surprised. Then they are upset. This is seldom good.

Make your banker an integral part of your team. You want them to be there for you when you need them.

OUTLINE OF BANK PRESENTATION

Refer to Appendix III for an outline of what should be included in a bank presentation.

SUMMARY

Few things are more important to your long-term success than financing your business properly and professionally. Analyze your debt requirements thoroughly and communicate this information clearly and concisely to your banker. Make sure you are well prepared when you make a presentation to the bank.

Your loans or line of credit at the bank are usually governed by a loan agreement that stipulates terms, interest rates, and covenants that restrict your ability to pay dividends and owner's salary or repay shareholder loans. Covenants may consist of a minimum current ratio, a minimum amount of working capital (current assets minus current liabilities), a maximum debt-to-equity ratio, or a minimum debt-coverage or interest-coverage ratio. *Make sure you understand what these covenants are and how they are calculated. Do not agree to a covenant that you know you cannot meet.*

There are four important rules to follow in your dealings with your banker:

1. Be prepared.
2. Establish a good personal relationship.
3. Keep your banker informed.
4. Never surprise your banker.

Take great pains to educate your banker about your business and answer any questions. Make sure everyone agrees about what is expected. Get it in writing. When problems arise, people tend to have selective memories about what was said. If you follow these rules of behavior with those who lend you money, your life will be a lot easier, and your reputation as a good businessperson will be greatly enhanced at the bank.

Allen got into financial trouble because he grew the company too fast. All of the trouble could have been avoided by regularly looking at a few financial relationships and communicating often with the banker.

Download *Business Mastery* from www.60minutecfo.com. Get the ratio averages for your industry from your banker or CPA or ask for them on my website and put them in the Ratios EOY tab. Use it to analyze your financial condition in comparison to others in your industry.

Prepare a forecast of your income statement, balance sheet, cash flow, and ratios and include it in your loan proposal. Become the first customer in the history of the bank to ever do such a thing. Be a star!

The next chapter will discuss how to get the most from your relationship with another financial member of your team, your CPA.

Keep it simple, and keep on paddling!

CHAPTER FOURTEEN: WORKING WITH YOUR CPA

14

INTRODUCTION

This book is about how to succeed in business, and one of the most important rules for success is to surround yourself with knowledgeable advisors. Selecting the right CPA, one who is knowledgeable in business accounting and your industry, is one of the most important business decisions you will make.

Do your research, ask other business owners for suggestions, and don't hesitate to ask prospective CPAs for references and their experience with companies in your industry. You need to hire a CPA who understands your needs and most important, communicates with you regularly and makes sure that you understand the information that is being provided to you.

TRADITIONAL VERSUS VALUE-ADDED SERVICE

Technical accounting knowledge is only one aspect of a good CPA. Traditionally, CPAs have acted as historians by providing financial information in the form of financial statements or tax returns. They may not have been concerned about whether you understood, or could interpret, the information they provided. If your business was experiencing difficulties, financial or otherwise, they likely would not comment on that.

Today, well-run CPA firms have a much broader perception of their roles in your business. They take a proactive approach to such things as an interpretation of your financial ratios and IRS regulations that may affect you. They examine and assist you with management information systems in your business and ownership-succession planning issues. In other words, the "green eyeshade number crunchers" of the past have been replaced by a new breed of CPAs who focus on helping businesses interpret and monitor financial information in a proactive way. This change in focus has changed the role of the CPA from just a *historian* to a trusted financial business *advisor*, and that is what you should expect from your CPA.

In the last twenty years, the accounting profession has grown more complex, and some firms have not kept up with changes in tax laws, financial reporting, and computerization. In the past, it was easier to be a generalist, but in today's environment, this is much more difficult.

If you are considering dealing with a large international firm, make sure that they have a division that is experienced in serving small and medium-sized businesses, and get references from firms that you interview.

ACCOUNTING SYSTEMS

The center of an accounting system is the general ledger (GL). Other components include accounts receivable (AR), accounts payable (AP), payroll, fixed assets, orders and billing, inventory, etc. The accounting system can be manual or computerized or a combination of both.

Many companies think that by having an expensive computer system, they have a good accounting system. Unfortunately, this is not always true. The accounting system is where financial transactions are recorded, monitored, and controlled. The computer may be the hub of the accounting system, but it is not responsible for making sure the entered transactions are accurate, properly controlled, and monitored. A poorly designed and monitored accounting system may allow fraud or unintentional errors to go undetected for years, and the loss to your business can be substantial before it is discovered.

Who is responsible for making sure your accounting system is operating properly? The CPA? Your controller or CFO? The ultimate answer to this question is that you and your CPA must make sure that any weaknesses are corrected in your business. Your CPA should be able to help you design and monitor your accounting system and its controls cost-effectively.

MONITORING THE SYSTEMS

Many businesses have complex accounting systems that are difficult to review properly, and some CPAs do not spend sufficient time testing underlying accounting systems, making sure that revenue and expenses are properly captured and recorded in the correct period. For most businesses, system testing is important, and owners should ask for a management letter from their CPA regarding any ideas or suggestions they might have.

Your CPA should play an important part in providing you with the assurance that your business's systems are operating appropriately, with adequate built-in controls. If you receive a reviewed or audited financial statement, make sure that you request a management letter, which discusses your accounting and management systems and controls. If you contract for a reviewed statement instead of an audited statement, your CPA will probably not be paying as much attention to your accounting system and controls unless you specifically ask that this is done.

LEVELS OF FINANCIAL STATEMENTS

COMPILED FINANCIAL STATEMENTS

The simplest form of financial statements that your CPA might provide you is called a *compiled* statement. These statements consist of placing the numbers that you generate internally on the letterhead of the accounting firm. In the process, the accountant looks at the statements and makes adjusting entries related to obvious errors.

Compiled financial statements are OK for most small firms but are typically not given too much credence by lenders for larger firms that require more substantial financing.

REVIEWED FINANCIAL STATEMENTS

In reviewed financial statements, the CPA makes general inquiries of management and performs some analytical procedures. Inquiries are made concerning key financial information. Analytical review procedures include a review of financial ratios, which are used to support the assertions of management and corroborate the answers to inquiries.

Although reviewed financial statements are substantially less in scope than an audit, they are well-received by the financial community for several reasons, including:

1. Reviewed statements hold the CPA to a higher level of responsibility than compiled statements.
2. The cost of a reviewed statement is much less than an audit.
3. The financial statements and related notes are more reliable.
4. Reviewed financial statements provide a good starting point for trend and cash flow analysis.
5. It shows a commitment by the owners to hold their organizations to higher standards of reporting.

Reviewed financial statements can also serve as an annual checkup of your accounting department. Through the inquiry process, your CPA may be able to determine if accounts have been reconciled and whether your accounting department is operating efficiently.

A reviewed statement can be a good start in helping a CPA understand your accounting systems. However, many CPAs do not extend their work beyond the required inquiries and analytical procedures. Make sure you ask about your CPA's procedures regarding your accounting system, and whether there are any recommendations because of their observations.

For many smaller firms under $1 million in revenue, compiled financial statements are satisfactory, but for larger and more complex firms that generate several million in revenue, a reviewed financial statement will be a more dependable document and will likely be required by the bank.

AUDITED FINANCIAL STATEMENTS

In an audit, the CPA performs specific audit procedures to determine whether your financial statements are in accordance with generally accepted accounting procedures (GAAP). The results of the audit are expressed in a letter of opinion that is issued by the CPA as a cover letter to the financial statements. An audit is in-depth and thus more expensive than a review or compilation. It includes detailed tests of account balances, testing of internal control procedures, and analytical review procedures designed to help provide the CPA with the necessary assurances to express an opinion, with the added benefit of helping the CPA understand your business.

Most businesses do not need audited financial statements, but some larger businesses must have an audit to satisfy banking requirements or shareholders not active in the business. Because of the expense involved, make sure you understand the reason for requiring an audit. At the cost of two to three times that of a review, you should always challenge the need for an audit.

In theory, the results presented in your financial statements, whether compiled, reviewed, or audited, should be the same. These statements should all conform to generally accepted accounting principles and include, in addition to the balance sheet and income statement, a statement of cash flow, retained earnings, and related notes.

The major differences between the various types of CPA-prepared financial statements are the accountant's opinion letter, the degree of verification of the information, the extensiveness of notes, and the cost.

Think about the level of financial statements that you need in your business and discuss this with your CPA.

TAX ISSUES

Taxation of businesses is complex and challenging. Your CPA needs to have adequate training and knowledge of your industry.

Your CPA should advise you as to whether you should elect *S* corporation status or remain a C corporation. If you are a C corporation and have never discussed this with your CPA, make sure you bring it up because there may be considerable benefits to you in electing *S* corporation status. If you are planning to sell your business, talk to your CPA *well in advance* about the tax issues you will face in this process.

Tax-planning discussions need to occur well before year-end. Planning is the most important part of reducing taxes, and proper tax planning can minimize the amount of tax that you must pay. Your CPA should be proactive in this process. Your year-end income tax liability should not be a surprise; it should be the by-product of proper advanced planning.

RULES FOR WORKING WITH YOUR CPA

Like working with your banker, as outlined in chapter thirteen, there are rules of behavior that you should follow when working with your CPA.

RULE NUMBER ONE: BE PROACTIVE AND ASK A LOT OF QUESTIONS

Your CPA provides services like an annual financial statement, tax return, and advice on estate planning. If they do not get any questions from you, they will assume that you understand everything that they have done.

Make sure that you ask questions every time they use a term you don't understand. If you don't understand the first answer, keep asking until you do. Communication is the key to obtaining satisfactory service from your CPA, and you should not hesitate to be proactive in this area.

Ask your CPA questions such as:

1. How am I doing, in your opinion?
2. How can I improve my accounting system?
3. What suggestions do you have for me to improve my profitability?

4. What are your thoughts about our industry and the economy for the coming year?
5. What should I be doing in the way of estate planning?
6. Do I have enough life insurance?
7. How can you help me interpret my financial performance and prepare a financial plan for next year?
8. Does my accounting staff have a good understanding and competence in their respective roles?

Your CPA wants to help you, but they are not mind readers. If you don't understand something or need help, ask for it.

RULE NUMBER TWO: GET YOUR CPA INVOLVED

Your CPA should be an integral member of your advisory team who will help you with a variety of issues, from establishing proper accounting systems to helping you plan for the long-term future of your business.

RULE NUMBER THREE: TALK REGULARLY

Be proactive and talk to your accountant at least once a quarter. Never assume that your accounting employees know all the answers to questions you might have or are performing their jobs correctly.

Checking and verifying your records and procedures regularly will save you much more money than it ever costs you in accounting fees.

RULE NUMBER FOUR: EXPECT GOOD SERVICE

Sometimes CPA firms become complacent about long-time clients, and the most responsive service is often oriented toward the newest clients.

Make sure that this doesn't happen to you and that you get good service. If you aren't receiving good service, let your CPA firm know that you're putting your job out for bids. This action will send the message that you expect them to be competitive and responsive, *or else.*

In many cases, you may be close friends with your CPA, but an experienced, qualified, involved, and responsive CPA firm is an integral part of your overall success, and you need to manage this relationship accordingly.

SUMMARY

The need for an outside CPA who understands your business is more important than ever, and your CPA should be able to assist you in navigating the complexities of today's business and tax environments. You are ultimately responsible for managing the relationship with your CPA. Ask for references. Request and expect timely service.

You and your controller or bookkeeper should meet with your CPA three to four times a year to discuss business in general and any questions or concerns you might have, especially regarding tax planning.

The CPA should prepare annual tax returns and financial statements and assist you with things like depreciation schedules, tax planning management systems and controls, and succession planning.

If you process payroll internally without using the services of an outside third-party firm, it is very important that you have your CPA review your procedures.

You are required to file several quarterly tax returns as well as annual filings, and it is important that you pay deposits for payroll taxes for both your firm and your employees when they are due. Failure to comply with these requirements can result in substantial fines and penalties, and your CPA is the one to help ensure that you comply in this area.

Your CPA is the best person, in addition to your banker, to help you understand, utilize, and implement the contents of this book, and should, therefore, be an important member of your advisory team.

The next chapter offers some tips on good leadership.

Keep it simple, and keep on paddling!

CHAPTER FIFTEEN: LEADERSHIP PRINCIPLES

15

INTRODUCTION

This is a book about business finance. It is intended to bridge the gap between business owners and their key financial advisors, but make no mistake, knowledge of business finance is not enough to guarantee success. Leadership is an important key to the success of the business. This chapter lists the top ten things that you need to practice, and the top ten things you should avoid to be a good leader. They are the result of observing the behavior of successful business owners over many years. Do your best to practice them on a day-to-day basis and share them with your leadership team. Hold fast to these principles, and you will be successful!

THE BIOLOGY OF LEADERSHIP

It turns out that there is a biological reason why good leadership promotes an atmosphere of success in a business. Cells in your brain define your behavior, action, thoughts, and memory. A positive experience helps create healthy brain cells, and stress or a negative environment has the opposite effect. If unabated a negative or stressful environment can cause an employee's brain to physically shrink in size, and the individual eventually sinks into depression and decreased productivity.

Leaders who nurture and create a positive environment can improve brain health among their employees and heal the brain cells that have been negatively impacted by periods of stress. Employees with healthy brains create a positive, efficient, and productive environment, which in turn attracts other people with healthy brains. Your company is soon cooking with positive, highly motivated, and productive people, and the negative, unproductive people have been weeded out. You get there with praise and a positive environment, not stress and criticism.

The following are the top ten things I have observed that good leaders do well. Learn and practice them every day, and you will have a happy and productive group of employees with healthy brains, and your company will enjoy greater success.

I.   INTEGRITY

These traits have not been listed in order of importance except for this one. Integrity is, by far the most important quality of a good leader. Integrity breeds trust, and when your employees know they can absolutely trust what you say and how you operate, it is a powerful thing. They'll respond favorably and do almost anything for you. Trust is fragile, easy to lose, and hard to obtain.

The amount of lying, cheating, and stealing that goes on in business today is disappointing. Dishonesty in business is so rampant that business schools now include classes in ethics—something that didn't exist in years past. Of course, you can't teach someone, to be honest; they either are, or they are not.

Good leaders have integrity. They play it straight with the company, its customers, employees, and the IRS. They *always* tell the truth. They say what needs to be said. They do not lie, cheat, or steal, even when there is a high probability that they won't be caught. Their employees trust them implicitly and tend to act in the same fashion.

Integrity is not a part-time thing, and you will never be a good leader without practicing it on a full-time basis.

> *You cannot maintain your integrity at 90% and be an effective leader. It's got to be 100%.* —**Leonard Roberts, CEO, the Tandy Co.**

II.   COMMUNICATION

Developing excellent communication skills is essential to effective leadership. The leader must be able to share knowledge and ideas to transmit a sense of urgency and enthusiasm to others. If a leader can't get a message across clearly and motivate others to act on it, then having a message doesn't even matter.

—Gilbert Amelio, CEO, National Semiconductor Corporation.

I believe that it is impossible to communicate too much. You will run out of time first. Good leaders are good communicators. They talk to people, and more important, they listen attentively. If something needs to be said, they say it. Comments on areas needing improvement are offered straightforwardly and constructively. Praise and compliments are offered freely and often. If leaders need help, advice, or suggestions, they ask for it. Recognition of significant achievements and important anniversaries is part of the culture of the company.

Communication leads to community, that is, to understanding, intimacy and mutual valuing. —Rollo **May, Psychologist, and author.**

III. COMPASSION

I don't care how much you know until I know how much you care. —**Steve Covey, 7 Habits of Highly Effective People**

Good leaders have compassion and demonstrate this often to their employees. When they learn that one of them has a critically ill spouse, as an example, they make a point of stopping by their workplace and asking how that spouse is getting along. They congratulate employees on their kid's soccer championship or other similar achievements. They tell them how much they appreciate the work they do. They honor them on important anniversaries. They frequently say, "thank you."

IV.   COURAGE

Courage is doing the things that you are afraid to do. There can be no courage unless you are scared. —**Eddie Rickenbacker, army aviator, and Medal of Honor winner.**

It takes courage to be in business. Every day you get up and put your financial well-being on the line. If you carry freight, every time you send a truck out on the road, you are one disastrous accident away from losing everything. If you are a carpet cleaner, every day that you put employees in people's homes, you hope that they will act appropriately and not expose you to legal or financial liability. It takes courage to own and run a business, and your employees need to look at you and see a calm and steady hand at the helm, especially when times get tough.

Courage means doing things that are tough to do, like letting go of a loyal and well-liked employee who has worked at the company for twenty-five years and is not willing to learn the complex technology required of the position. Courage is sitting down with a son who does not have the right work ethic or aptitude and telling him he can no longer work in the family business.

Good leaders face these types of situations when they arise and take appropriate action.

V. ATTITUDE

I never failed at anything, I've just found ten thousand ways that don't work. —**Thomas Edison**

You need to be the company's biggest cheerleader, no matter how dire the situation. Let your enthusiasm for your work permeate down to your employees. Whether you think you can, or you think you can't, you're right. There is no substitute for a positive attitude.

Lou Piniella, successful Major League Baseball manager, said it this way:

> *It's easier to lose than it is to win. Winning is difficult. Everyone wants to win. It's just that every person when they're not winning, doesn't want to dig a little deeper, play a little harder, a little smarter. Winning is an attitude, and what you have to do is develop an attitude for your team that winning is the most important thing. You look at teams that win—all the players are successful. It's all tied together.*

Develop an attitude for your team that winning (being successful) is the most important thing. Never deviate from this.

When the odds against you are a million to one, focus on the one. **Aaron Baker, a quadriplegic who learned to walk and run again.**

Attitude is everything.

VI. VISION

A good hockey player plays the puck where it is. A great hockey player plays the puck where it is going to be. —**Wayne Gretzky**

Great leaders have a great vision. You cannot achieve anything of significance unless you mentally see it first. No wood carver ever carved a beautiful sculpture without visualizing it first. Without a vision for your company, there is no direction. No one understands what you're trying to do and how they might help you.

A leader must provide a vision—clear and achievable 'big ideas' combined in a strategic concept—and communicate those ideas throughout the entire organization and to all other stakeholders. —**General David Petraeus**

VII. HUMILITY

Oh, lord, it's hard to be humble when you're perfect in every way. — **Mac Davis, It's hard to be humble lyrics.**

Business owners and CEOs are held in high esteem. They are treated with deference and respect, and employees know that they have pretty much complete power over their employment and financial well-being. Unfortunately, they often begin to believe their press clippings and consequently lose touch with their employees.

Good leaders understand that success is always a result of a team effort rather than that of one person. They know that it's amazing how much you can accomplish when you don't care who gets the credit. "It is the team that succeeded not me," they say, and they are right. Employees expect the boss to take all the credit and are surprised and pleased when that is not the case.

Fullness of knowledge always and necessarily means some understanding of the depths of our ignorance, and that is always conducive to both humility and reverence. **Robert A. Millikan, Nobel laureate physicist.**

VIII. CONSISTENCY

There are those who would misteach us that to stick in a rut is consistency —and a virtue, and that to climb out of the rut is inconsistency and a vice. —**Mark Twain**

Good leaders can be counted on to have a set of values they follow consistently. This quality acts as a stabilizing force, without which the internal workings of a company can be easily disrupted when faced with challenges.

Consistency of purpose is not to be confused with inflexibility; rather it provides a firmness of character and allows a company to be ready for the changes and difficult decisions that will inevitably occur in the ordinary course of business. Core values define what a company and its employees stand for and who they are. They are what drive the company.

It is not difficult for good leaders to be consistent. It is part of who they are. Chris Petersen, a highly successful Division I college football coach, put it this way after he benched a star defensive player for committing a personal foul:

> *I'm just not into stupid penalties. It's not even an issue whether the guy's going to play or not if they don't conduct themselves right. If you don't play like we want you to play, you're not playing. It's not even a decision for me; it's easy.*

Good leaders set high standards for profitability, performance, and overall excellence in all operations of the business and never deviate from those standards. They have core values and stick to them, and employees know that they can count on this stability and consistency in the company.

IX.   BALANCE

We have all experienced the alpha CEO. Their smartphones provide twenty-four/seven accessibility and are never far from reach. Their phone comes to meetings, the dinner table, the bedroom, and e-mails answered at ten o'clock on a Sunday evening with great pride.

These are serious, dedicated, hardworking, conscientious people who check out the parking lot on Saturday morning to see whose car is not there. Work is everything to these people, and they know that to be successful, you must be dedicated and willing to make sacrifices. If you must miss the kid's baseball game or recital, so be it. Well, no.

Good leaders realize that to be truly successful, they must have balanced lives. Time with family and service to the community are priorities. If a CEO needs to be available twenty-four seven for the business to be successful, then there is a serious delegation and leadership problem. The smartphone does not have to be surgically attached to a hand. This is an addiction, much like any other, and it should not be allowed or tolerated.

Make sure there is a balance in your life as well as in the lives of your employees. As the old saying goes, few people on their deathbeds say, "I wish I had spent more time at the office."

X.   KNOWLEDGE OF FINANCE

Of course, I am going to include a knowledge of finance in the top ten. That's what this book is about, but most owners or managers businesses do not have a background in finance. This lack of knowledge results in conversations with controllers, bankers, CPAs, or financial consultants that can be confusing or even annoying. Financial people often speak in their own "language," and use terms that are technical and not always understood. This book takes that language and describes it in plain English so that anyone with a non-financial background can understand it.

The prior chapters contain all the information you need to understand business finance, and the good news is that all you need is sixty minutes a month to make it all work!

LEADERSHIP TRAITS TO AVOID

Now let's take a look at what business owners don't do well.

I.   FAILURE TO ACT PROMPTLY

When revenue declines the first inclination by many is to work harder, generate more leads, and increase the closing ratios of the salespeople. The hope is that the decline temporary or that it can be reversed quickly. This is where the problem begins because few companies are successful at selling themselves out of trouble.

When revenue declines, you need to take a hard look at expenses and cut them as much as necessary to maintain profit margins. Determine what expenses can easily be eliminated and do it right away. If more cuts are necessary, sit down with your management team and decide which employees should be laid off. Laying people off is not fun, but it is part of running a successful and profitable business.

II.   TOLERATING MEDIOCRITY

The second biggest thing I have observed is putting up with poor performance, sometimes for years. The fact is that every business has A, B, and C employees. The As are exceptional; the Bs are average and generally meet expectations; and the Cs are marginal, but not bad enough to be fired.

You need to sit down with the Cs and tell them specifically what is expected to continue working for you. The message is clear, they either improve, or they are gone. Failing to do this sends a very bad message to all of your A and B employees and it is bad for morale. This impact is especially true if the C employee is a family member.

The fact is that A employees attract and hire other A employees, and it is not long before you have an exceptional group of high achievers in your company. Weed out the Cs promptly and send the clear message that mediocrity is not acceptable.

III.   LACK OF FOCUS

Successful leaders have a *laser beam* focus on such things as goals, standards of behavior, and core values. Even the slightest deviations from prescribed procedures and standards are immediately mentioned and corrected. Employees are much like kids; they will test you to see if you are serious. Make sure your employees know what is expected and then never fail to make corrections when necessary.

IV.   FAILURE TO ASK FOR HELP

If the company has a problem such as not achieving projected profit margins, the first thing you need to do is assemble your management team and ask for their help in correcting this. Avoid the temptation to start making decisions about what needs to be done by yourself. A successful business will *always* be the result of a team effort.

V.   FAILURE TO AUDIT EXPENSES

Periodically you need to sit down with your controller or accounting manager and go over every dollar that is being spent. Every single dollar. I have never seen a case where this did not yield at least a ten percent reduction in expenses. It's called zero-based budgeting. If you fail to do this, it is virtually certain that you are spending too much. If you don't care how much you are spending, then neither will your employees.

VI.   FAILURE   TO   HOLD   PEOPLE ACCOUNTABLE

Chapters seven through ten outline how to prepare a business plan, but nothing will be accomplished unless people are held accountable. High achieving A employees do not mind this at all. They *expect* to be held accountable. If someone is having difficulty achieving a stated goal, then find out the reason and work with that person until the situation is resolved.

VII.   FAILURE TO HAVE A PLAN B.

Everyone has a plan till they get punched in the mouth. —**Mike Tyson, philosopher and former heavyweight world champion.**

In 2008, a lot of business owners got punched in the mouth. The U.S. economy, hit by a huge international financial crisis, was in freefall. The country experienced the worst recession since the Great Depression, and Plan A was clearly not going to work for most businesses. In 2020

COVID 19 dealt another body blow. When this happens, you need to have a Plan B, which you do if Plan A does not work.

Have Plan B already drawn up and documented in detail so that it can be implemented quickly. Keep it up-to-date as you work on Plan A. Plan A assumes the best, and Plan B plans for the worst.

VIII. FAILURE TO THINK STRATEGICALLY

There are a lot of companies that have failed because of the lack of thinking strategically, and you should observe and learn from them.

EXAMPLE: KODAK

Kodak invented the digital camera and then shelved it because they felt it would hurt their film business. Then it went bankrupt.

EXAMPLE: GENERAL MOTORS

General Motors basically ignored the competitive threat from some foreign automakers and management arrogantly felt that they would always dominate the auto market as they had for over 70 years. Then it went bankrupt.

The tendency for many is to do things "the way they have always been done," but good leaders never assume that the status quo is always going to be successful. They are constantly on the alert for changes in the market, the environment, or technology that could be a threat to their company. They think strategically and recognize threats or opportunities for their business in time to take necessary action. Every day is day one. Ignore these challenges at your peril.

IX. FAILURE TO PRAISE INSTEAD OF CRITICIZE

Criticizing rather than praising is standard behavior that many in a leadership position follow. You see something being done incorrectly and you mention it. You know that employees will test you, and if you are not diligent, employees will eventually realize that the rules of performance and behavior are not important and don't need to be followed. The more observant and critical you are, the better everyone will perform. If someone asks why you never praise good performance, your answer is, "Why should I praise someone for doing what I pay them to do?"

The reason you should be quick to praise instead of criticizing is very simple. People respond better to praise than to criticism. If you see someone in the warehouse looking nice and wearing a clean company uniform, why not mention it? "Sam, you are looking sharp today. Thanks for making us look good!" Sam is not likely to forget that the boss told him he looked good, and he is going to focus on getting another compliment like that.

Praise makes people feel happy. It makes them realize that someone notices that they are doing a good job. It makes them want to keep doing a good job so that they will continue to get praise.

If you do have to point out a shortcoming, try to phrase it in a positive way. "Ted, we have had customers tell us how impressed they are with our warehouse, but I've noticed some scrap lumber and material laying around lately. Let's make sure we always deserve their praise." Ted will get the idea and be motivated to deserve complements in the future.

You should never miss an opportunity to praise those around you and thank them for being such a great help to the company. They will try even harder in the future to earn your praise.

X. FAILURE TO DELEGATE

Many business owners subscribe to the theory that if you want something done right, you must do it yourself. No one else is going to have the high standards and expertise that you have, and it is easier to do the job than it is to try and train someone else to do it.

Employees come into your office with a particularly difficult task they are working on, and it is tempting to offer to help them out and complete it for them. Monkey off the employee, and monkey on the boss. It does not take long to learn that the boss will do their job for them.

A failure to delegate ultimately means that there is a huge bottleneck at the top of the company. Nothing is operating at peak efficiency, and, worse yet, no one is being trained to alleviate this situation in the future.

Ego may affirm that no one can do the job as well as you can, but this is folly. You need to put people in positions of responsibility, give them the authority to perform, and then hold them accountable. Realize that they will make mistakes and learn from them. Delegation is the only way to build a strong and prosperous business that is not dependent on one or two people.

SUMMARY

The most successful and well-run companies are consistently profitable, in prosperity or recession. They do not tolerate losing.

The owners of those successful businesses are probably not smarter, more experienced, or more knowledgeable than less successful business owners, but they are good leaders, and they adhere to the principles in this chapter. Make sure that you do not hide behind the economy, status of the industry, or seasonality as an excuse for losing money. It's not valid in most instances, and you can avoid losses by adhering to the principles listed above.

I have spent the last thirty-plus years observing the leadership characteristics of successful companies. I can attest that if you religiously apply the principles in this chapter, you will likely never lose money.

The next chapter will offer some tips on starting a new business.

Keep it simple, and keep on paddling!

Studies have shown that paddling a canoe makes you more awesome than the general population.

CHAPTER SIXTEEN: TIPS ON STARTING A BUSINESS

16

STARTING VERSUS RUNNING A BUSINESS

This book is about how to run a successful and profitable business, but if you are reading it before starting your own business, some comments about what all is entailed in the startup process are appropriate.

Entrepreneurs start businesses. That's what they do. When it comes to *running* the business, they are bored and want to move on to the next business to start. They are not well-suited to running, leading, and operating a successful business. Boring. The fun and excitement are in starting the business.

Entrepreneurs typically start businesses in their thirties. They don't know enough in their twenties, and they know *too much* in their forties.

They know how to make, do, or sell something, and they have confidence in their abilities and vision. They have little money, no fear, and lots of energy. They *know* they are going to succeed and are willing to work 24/7, if necessary, to make it happen.

A hairdresser that wants to open a salon can form a corporation or limited liability company (LLC) with standard forms available online. Then lease some inexpensive space, purchase a few used chairs, get a plumber to install some sinks, design a website; light up Facebook, Twitter and Linked-In with your new venture, and presto, you are in the hairdressing business. It might be a little more complicated than that for some, but technology and the Internet have taken a lot of the pain and expense out of the intricacies of starting a business. The problem is that *running* a hairdressing business is a lot more difficult than *starting* a business, and survival statistics are not encouraging.

HIGH FAILURE RATE

Approximately 80 percent of all businesses fail within the first fifteen years. Most of those failures are not because the idea or product lacked sufficient demand, or the hairdresser couldn't cut hair; they are due to *bad management.*

Running a business may look easy when you are working for someone else, but it is not. This is especially true if you don't know and understand the leadership/management process or the financial management side of the business that are discussed in this book. Entrepreneurs with skill, vision, and energy usually do not have any experience in running a business, and they are often not good at it. Running a successful business is a lifetime learning process that never ends, and it takes both hard work and a good grasp of the complexities involved to succeed.

PRIMARY REASONS FOR FAILURE

LACK OF PLANNING.

This is the big one. Entrepreneurs tend not to be great planners. They are action-oriented people who focus on the tasks at hand rather than one or two years ahead. The three most important aspects of starting a business are planning, planning, and planning. See chapters seven through ten of this book for a detailed discussion on how to establish a plan for your new business.

LACK OF TIMELY AND ACCURATE FINANCIAL INFORMATION.

Hiring professionals to keep your books can be expensive but handing a shoebox full of receipts to your bookkeeper or CPA at the end of the year is not a good idea and is a poor way to save money. Inexpensive and easy-to-use accounting programs are available today so that even laypeople can produce monthly financial statements.

Hire a good bookkeeper and pay a consultant to set up your chart of accounts. Make sure you get and understand financial statements monthly. This is not complicated, but it does take a little effort and learning on your part. See chapters one through four for a detailed discussion on how to properly analyze your financial statements. Refer to chapter fourteen for a discussion about dealing with your CPA.

FAILURE TO UNDERSTAND AND TRACK CASH FLOW.

Cash is king. You pay your bills, employees, and debts with cash. You pay for nothing with profits. As a beginning business owner, your sole focus is on becoming profitable, and profits are not synonymous with cash flow. You need to understand this and know why, and not a single number on your financial statements pertain to cash flow. See chapter four for a detailed discussion on analyzing cash flow.

LACK OF UNDERSTANDING OF HOW TO MANAGE DEBT.

Business owners who have a great idea, great skills and supreme confidence have a hard time understanding a lender's unwillingness to loan them money. They have no capital, no revenue, no profits, no cash flow, and no history of profitability and are perplexed when they are politely but firmly turned down at the bank. Really? Entrepreneurs tend to believe that sufficient loans are all they need to succeed. Not.

When revenue and profits grow in the early stages of the business, they see this as good. When debt goes up to support the increase in revenue, they view this as OK and a conventional part of the growing process. The increase in debt may or may not be OK. See chapters one and five for more information on how to manage debt, and chapter thirteen in dealing with your banker.

FAILURE TO KNOW COSTS.

Most new business owners have little or no idea of what the costs are to produce or sell their products or services. Pricing is, therefore, unsophisticated and may not allow for sufficient profit margins. Even veteran business owners, who have been in business for many years, tend to let competitive forces dictate pricing strategies. This is rarely optimal. You need to analyze and know your costs and then set your pricing strategies accordingly. See chapters two and eleven for a detailed discussion about this.

FAILURE TO TRANSITION FROM SEAT OF THE PANTS (SOP) MANAGEMENT TO PROFESSIONAL MANAGEMENT.

Starting a business is an interesting process. The focus is solely on the founder and his or her vision. There is neither the money nor the need to hire a big staff, so management is largely a solo effort. There is no formal organization chart with written job descriptions. Everyone reports to the owner and everyone does whatever needs doing. Decisions are made on the fly, without the involvement or need for multiple layers of management or committees. The workday is not an 8:00 a.m. to 5:00 p.m. environment. You work as many hours as necessary to get the business going. It is an all-consuming exercise. It's hard work, but it is also fun and exciting.

Entrepreneurs, by their very nature and skills, are good at *starting* a business, but not good at *running* one. Seat-of-the-pants (SOP) management, applicable at the outset, falters badly as the business grows and needs more sophisticated leadership, systems, and procedures, all a serious pain in the butt to the entrepreneur. Delegation and teamwork become necessary. A more formal structure, with an organizational chart and job descriptions, is required. Individual egos need to be set aside as the leadership team becomes more important than one person.

The founder hates this onset of bureaucracy and chafes at these developments. Gone are the good old freewheeling days. There are many examples of founders of companies who were eventually dismissed as the CEO by an unhappy board of directors (Steve Jobs more than once) because they failed to transition to professional management. Few people are comfortable changing management styles, and for a small business, this almost always becomes a serious problem.

The combined result of the above shortcomings is often the failure of the business. Learn the financial and leadership principles discussed in this book. Don't rely on luck or good timing. Prepare and educate yourself for success in the long-term.

This book is not about how to *make, sell,* or *do* something. That is knowledge that you already have or can get from specialized publications. This is a book on how to *run* a successful business. Read it and keep it handy. Don't resist transitioning to more formal leadership when it is necessary—embrace it. I can tell you from personal experience, you won't like having the increased formality, but not making this transition is a recipe for disaster as your company grows. Your business will become chaotic at a critical time when it will have the worst impact on your business.

CHECKLIST FOR STARTING A BUSINESS.

You have an idea and a vision. You have thought about it for months or even years, and you decide to pull the trigger, eager to get going. Careful preparation takes a back seat as you fearlessly dive into the deep end of the pool and either learn to swim or drown. Preparation and planning are tedious. You want to get going on this journey.

The following is a checklist of what needs to be done *before* you start a business. Make sure you check everything off before you begin. What starts out wrong ends up wrong and following these steps can help to ensure that you start out right.

WRITE YOUR BUSINESS PLAN.

If you don't know how to do it, read this book or any of the multitude of books that are available on this subject. Google "business plan," and you will find more material than you can absorb. Do your homework. Get assistance from people you trust. Go to the Small Business Association (SBA) and get free consulting from retired business executives who have the knowledge and experience that you lack. This is the first and most important step in starting a business. See chapters seven through ten for information on the planning process. Refer to Appendix II for a listing of what should be included in a business plan.

DETERMINE YOUR FINANCIAL REQUIREMENTS.

Determining your financial requirements is part of the business plan, but it needs special mention. How soon will you break-even (where revenue is at least equal to, or greater than expenses), and how much will you lose before you do? Refer to chapter eleven for a discussion on this. Calculating your break-even revenue will help you determine how much money you will need to start the business. Then you need to figure out the source of that money.

Optimism usually prevails in this process, but the rule-of-thumb is that *it usually takes twice as long and twice as much money to achieve your initial forecasts.* Plan for this at the outset. Think about the worst-case scenario. Hope for the best and plan for the worst.

Initial capital is probably going to have to come from your savings, money you raise by selling or mortgaging your home, the money you borrow from friends and family, and a lot of "sweat equity." Do not assume that traditional sources of equity or debt are going to be available to you. Maybe they will be but hope for the best and plan for the worst.

Raising money through an angel investor or venture capitalist is beyond the scope of this book, but if you are planning to go that route, you need experienced legal and financial advice. You can wind up with significant financial liabilities if this is not done correctly. It is *not* a do-it-yourself project.

Remember the four Fs in searching for start-up money: Founders, Family, Friends, and Fools. Look for money in that order, and please, if you have aging, retired parents, do not ask them for a loan unless they are very well off. It is not a time in their lives when they should be risking their retirement savings.

Get *Business Mastery*, an Excel-based workbook for financial analysis, and forecasting from www.60minutecfo.com. Use it to make a range of forecasts for your business; best case, worst case, most likely case, etc.

COMPLETE THE LEGAL REQUIREMENTS.
Your choice for the form of your business is realistically limited to a *C* corporation; an *S* corporation; or a limited liability company (LLC). Other options include a partnership or sole proprietorship, but these forms do not limit the liability of the owners. Each form of business has pros and cons, so do your homework to determine what is best for your

business. Make sure the proposed name of your company is available and register it with the secretary of state where you live. Get federal and state tax ID numbers and the necessary business licenses and permits. Do your research on what is required and consult an experienced business attorney for advice when needed.

Make sure you have appropriate articles of incorporation, bylaws, operating agreements, and shareholder agreements. Know and understand what they say. If you don't understand parts of these documents, keep asking questions until you do. There may be a dizzying amount of fine print or boilerplate that appears to be benign, but it is important for you to have a good grasp of the legal foundation of your company and understand what these documents contain. Take the time to go over them thoroughly and ask enough questions to make sure you understand what they say.

You should know and understand your legal responsibilities as an employer, especially your payroll tax and medical insurance responsibilities. Open the necessary bank accounts. There is a lot of information available on all of this, but it is not your expertise. Invest in the advice of a good lawyer and CPA at the outset. It is part of the start-up capital that you require.

WRITE YOUR MARKETING PLAN.
Who are you going to sell to and how? How big is the market? Who are your competitors? What are the opportunities for growth? What is your market niche? What, if any, is your competitive advantage? What is your pricing strategy? What marketing material are you going to need, who is going to design it, and how much will it cost? What is your advertising

plan? Sales and marketing may come easily to you, but if not, get some help.

ESTABLISH YOUR EQUIPMENT NEEDS.

What furniture, equipment, and vehicles will you need? How much will this cost? Don't overlook things like computers and phone systems. Research this and make sure that the equipment you plan to acquire is satisfactory for your needs.

ESTABLISH YOUR STAFFING PLAN.

Who will you need? When? What will you have to pay? What training will they need and who will do it? How will they be managed and by whom?

ESTABLISH YOUR PRODUCTION PLAN.

Who, when, where, and how?

PLAN FOR THE WORST.

What are the things that can go wrong? What are the risk factors? What are the soft spots in your plan? What are the reasons why you should abandon this project? Examining what might go wrong is the opposite thinking of anyone who has ever started a business.

Entrepreneurs are optimistic people who believe that they *will not fail*. They believe that nothing can go wrong. Optimism overflows. Confidence is supreme. This optimistic thinking is good, but don't avoid trying to find the weak points in your plan. Carefully examine *all* the potential risk factors and what might go wrong. Challenge every aspect of your plan. Hope for the best and plan for the worst.

SUMMARY

Hopefully you will beat the odds and succeed, but a wise person considers all contingencies. Every venture has risk factors, and you should spare no effort in determining what they might be for your start-up venture.

Approach starting a business with extreme skepticism, and never think that it is a "sure thing." Remember the statistics—80 percent of all businesses fail within fifteen years. Think of all the ways that this might happen to you. Most of those failures are avoidable with careful planning.

Careful research and planning, along with obtaining expert professional advice, will go a long way toward preventing you from being one of the 80 percent casualties. Remember that *starting* a business is a lot easier than *running* it. Read the rest of this book for information on how to run a successful business. Then re-read it. Keep it handy and refer to it regularly. It is the only way that this information will eventually be part of your consciousness and become second nature to you.

Running a successful business is hard work, but it is also fun. Parts of it can be complex, but it does not need to be mysterious. Read carefully the chapters of this book that cover areas in which you have the least knowledge. Careful adherence to the financial and leadership principles discussed in this book will result in success and sustained profitability, and that should be your goal.

The next chapter offers some final thoughts on operating a successful business.

Keep it simple, and keep on paddling!

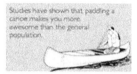

CHAPTER SEVENTEEN: CONCLUSION

17

It is possible to learn the basics of business finance in 60 minutes. It takes less than that amount of time to read the first four chapters of this book that describe what you need to know in plain English. It is not possible, however, to retain this knowledge without reviewing it monthly. Without a regular review, this information will gradually fade away. You will forget what the current ratio is and why you are looking at it.

The solution is to give it 60 minutes a month. Input your monthly financial statements into *Business Mastery* and go over this information with your leadership team. Re-read the first four chapters once a month to remind yourself what each ratio means and why you need to look at it. No one ever gets proficient in anything without working at it, and understanding business finance basics is no exception.

This book is about how to run a successful business, but always remember that one person does not achieve success. It is always a team effort, and good leaders understand this. They surround themselves with smart, well-trained people who manage the key areas of their business. They delegate duties and responsibilities to their key managers and hold them accountable for results.

Good leaders hire people who are smarter than they are (at least in some areas) who want to be part of a winning team. They do not settle for mediocrity. They either coach up unproductive employees or graciously allow them to offer their services elsewhere.

Leading a successful business is a journey and not a destination. It is a lifetime learning proposition, and it is helpful to observe others in a leadership capacity and determine what they do well and what they do not do as well. You can do this within your industry as you meet and observe other owners, and you can also do this by observing leaders of public companies, or coaches of traditionally successful athletic teams.

A great example of a leader to pattern yourself after is Alan Mulally, former CEO of Ford Motor Company. Showing great courage, he left a good job at the Boeing Company, where he was credited with heroic-like performance, and took the reins of a virtually bankrupt Ford Motor Company. He installed a winning culture and built a team of executives who were successful in saving the company and preserved hundreds of thousands of jobs in the process. Read the book on how he did it (refer to the bibliography), and then try to be just like Alan.

A leader you might not want to emulate is Steve Jobs, former CEO of Apple (see the bibliography for a book about him). Steve had great vision, but by all other accounts, he was not a nice or compassionate person. He was sometimes arrogant, rude, and often mean to those around him. He was not a good leader, and Apple dismissed him as the CEO on more than one occasion. His vision may be credited with preserving Apple, which is a great legacy, but he was not a gifted leader.

Keep this book close by, and occasionally re-read a chapter. Give a copy of this book to all your leadership team members and review parts of it regularly. Better yet, have your key people *teach* parts of it in your monthly management meetings. People learn what they teach, and this information needs to be reviewed regularly until it becomes second nature, or you will lose it.

Nothing is more powerful than a leadership team that understands the financial concepts and are pulling in the same harness, in the same direction and working together to make success happen, and this includes both your banker and CPA.

So here you are, a little further along on your journey in the canoe. You are stronger for having paddled this far, but you and other key members of your business must keep working and learning. It is a life-long process. And no, we are not there yet. So, keep on paddling!

Best wishes to you for a safe, successful, and enjoyable journey,
David A. Duryee
2021

APPENDIX I: AVAILABLE WORKBOOKS

The following is a list of the available Excel-based workbooks that accompany this book. Download them at www.60minutecfo.com.

Business Mastery:
Use this workbook to analyze your annual and monthly financial statements, as well as forecasting income statement, balance sheet, cash flow, and financial ratios.

Business Break-Even:
Use this workbook to calculate the break-even revenue for your business as well as revenue necessary to make a specified net profit. Refer to chapter eleven.

Business Equipment:
Use this workbook to determine if it makes sense to purchase a vehicle or piece of equipment.

Business Review:
Use this workbook to rate your business using a comprehensive checklist.

APPENDIX II: BUSINESS PLAN OUTLINE

I. **Executive Summary**

    A. A one-page summary of the business, history, and summary of the prior year, any changes anticipated, financing required, etc.

II. **Company Description**

    A. Company profile—a paragraph describing your company, owners, legal form, etc.

    B. List of key management and advisors.

    C. Current year summary—actual performance versus plan, goals achieved, etc.

    D. The outlook for the coming year—economy, industry, and company.

    E. Financial summary—revenue, profits, and key ratios for the past three years.

    F. Core values—what values drive the company?

    G. Vision statement—what the company will look like at the end of three years.

    H. Mission statement—why are you in business?

    I. List of company strengths, competitive advantages, and core competencies.

    J. Organizational chart—who reports to whom?

    K. Total staff count and staff levels for administration, sales, operations, production, etc.

III. **Strategic goals and objectives**

    List the primary goals that you hope to accomplish for the coming year, the persons responsible, and their deadlines.

IV. **Sales and marketing plan**

    A. Lines of business you hope to grow and how that will be accomplished.

    B. Sales goals by product line and market area.

        C.   Competitive pressures.

        D.   Pricing strategies.

        E.   Lead generation programs.

        F.   Marketing plan—advertising, collateral material, community involvement, chamber of commerce, etc.

        G.   New products/services, if any, that will be offered and the plan for doing that.

V.   Financial Plan

        A.   Forecasted income statement, including supporting assumptions.

        B.   Forecasted balance sheet.

        C.   Forecasted cash flow.

        D.   Forecasted ratios.

        E.   Capital expenditure plan—equipment, timing, and planned financing.

VI.   Facilities plan

        A.   Expansion necessary.

        B.   Major repairs planned.

        C.   Lease renewals required.

VII.   Staff plan: new hires and planned layoffs

APPENDIX III: BANK PROPOSAL OUTLINE

I. Proposal
   A. XYZ, Inc. is seeking the following bank accommodations:
   1. $750,000 revolving line of credit utilizing accounts receivable as collateral.
   2. $1,000,000 equipment term-loan line of credit secured by equipment.
   B. Proceeds will be used for seasonal cash flow needs and purchase of equipment.

II. Overview
   A. Description of the business
   Form of business (C Corp, S Corp, or LLC), owners, date started, locations, the board of directors, vision statement, mission statement, core values
   B. Key officers and management; position, experience, tenure, age
   C. Organization chart
   D. Key advisors: legal, accounting, insurance, advisory board, etc.
   E. Description of insurance coverage

III. Description of market and products
   A. Business lines as a percentage of revenue
   B. Major customers
   C. Market size
   D. Market share
   E. Primary competition
   F. Description of sales and marketing strategy

IV. Description of facilities
   Size, location, condition, capacity, etc.

V. Financial
   A. Three years of income statements
   B. Three years of balance sheets
   C. Three years of cash flow
   D. Three years of financial ratios, use *Business Mastery*
   E. Forecasted income statement, balance sheet, statement of cash flow, and ratios, use *Business Mastery*

F. Copy of most recent tax return

G. Comments on financial condition and forecast

VI. Strategic Goals and Objectives for the year

Appendixes

1. Owner resumes
2. References
3. Shareholder agreement, if any
4. Equipment list – model, year, cost, estimated value
5. List of existing leases/contracts
6. By-laws and articles of incorporation, LLC operating agreement

APPENDIX IV: SUMMARY OF FINANCIAL RATIOS

Ratio	Measures	Reference
Current ratio	Liquidity	Chap 1
Debt-to-equity ratio	Safety/Risk	Chap 1
Gross profit margin	Profit level one	Chap 2
Operating profit margin	Profit level two	Chap 2
Net profit margin	Profit level three	Chap 2
Return on equity	Reward	Chap 3
Receivable days	# of days in accounts receivable	Chap 3
Inventory days	# of days in inventory	Chap 3
Payable days	# of days to pay bills	Chap 3
Survival score	Overall financial health	Chap 3
Rev. per admin. emp.	Number of admin staff	Chap 3
Oper. cash flow margin	Oper. Cash flow ÷ revenue	Chap 4
Financing cash flow margin	Fin. Cash flow ÷ revenue	Chap 4
Net cash flow margin	Net cash flow ÷ revenue	Chap 4

GLOSSARY

Accounts payable

A current liability representing the amount owed to trade creditors for merchandise or services purchased on open account (i.e., without giving a note or other evidence of debt).

Accounts payable period (days)

Expressed in days, it represents the length of time it typically takes to pay trade creditors. This is calculated by dividing cost of goods sold by accounts payable, which is equal to accounts payable turnover, and then dividing 365 by this turnover. If the period being measured is not a year, then the cost of goods sold should be annualized before making this calculation.

Accounts receivable

A current asset representing money owed for merchandise or services sold on open account.

Accounts receivable aging

Grouping accounts receivable according to due dates that represent the length of time an account has been outstanding, such as:
    0–30 days
    31–60 days
    61–90 days
    Over 90 days

Accounts receivable collection period also known as receivable days or days' sales outstanding (DSO)

Expressed in days, it represents the length of time it typically takes to collect accounts receivable. This is calculated by dividing revenue by accounts receivable, which is equal to accounts receivable turnover, and then dividing 365 by this turnover. If the period being measured is not a year, then revenue should be annualized before making this calculation.

Accrual-basis accounting

The practice of record-keeping by which revenue is recorded when earned, and expenses are recorded when incurred, even though cash may not be received or paid out until later. This is opposed to cash-basis accounting, which only recognizes revenue when cash is received, or expenses when cash is paid.

Accrued expenses
A current liability representing expenses incurred during a fiscal period, but not actually paid by the end of that fiscal period.

Accumulated depreciation
Also referred to as allowance or reserve for depreciation. The total of all depreciation taken on a fixed asset since its purchase.

Administrative expenses
Also referred to as general and administrative expenses (G&A), operating expenses, indirect expenses, or overhead. These expenses typically include utilities, advertising, legal, accounting, travel, entertainment, administrative salaries, office expenses, professional fees, taxes and licenses, etc.

Amortization expense
The gradual write-off of an intangible asset, such as copyright or goodwill, over a period of years. It is a noncash charge against earnings, like depreciation.

Appreciation
The increase in the value of an asset in excess of its cost or book value, which is due to economic and other conditions.

Asset
Anything owned by an individual or a business. Assets may consist of specific property or claims against others. Assets are reflected on the balance sheet at the lower of cost or current value.

Bad debts
The amounts due on open accounts that have been proven uncollectible.

Balance sheet
An itemized statement of all the assets, liabilities, and equity of an individual or business at a given point in time. It is known as a position statement.

Balance sheet spread
The organization of several years of balance sheets on one piece of paper for ease of analysis of trends and calculation of financial ratios.

Book value
The value of the assets, liabilities, and equity as reflected on the balance sheet. The book value of a business is determined by deducting total liabilities from total assets. The book value of the assets of a company may have little or no relationship to the actual fair market value of the assets.

Break-even point
The point at which revenue and expenses are equal. A combination of revenue and expenses that will yield zero net profit.

Budget
An itemized listing of the amount of all estimated revenue that a given business anticipates receiving and the listing and segregation of the amount of all estimated expenses that will be incurred in obtaining the income during a given period, such as a month, a year, etc.

Capital
The amount of money invested in the business by shareholders. It consists of the initial stock investment and retained earnings. It is also referred to as equity or net worth.

Capital assets
A term that includes all fixed assets, consisting of vehicles, furniture and fixtures, land, buildings, machinery, etc.

Capital budgeting
The practice of allocating funds set aside for investment in fixed assets in the most effective manner. It takes into consideration the risks and possible returns of various potential investments. It is the process of determining whether an asset should be purchased based upon its estimated generated cash flows. It is the process of planning expenditures for capital (fixed) assets.

Capital gain or loss
The gain or loss between the book value and sale price of a capital (fixed) asset.

Capital stock
The shares of a corporation authorized by its articles of incorporation, including preferred and common stocks.

Cash-basis accounting
The practice of recording income and expenses only when cash is received or paid out. This is opposed to accrual-basis accounting, which recognizes revenue when items or services are sold and expenses when they are incurred, versus when they are paid.

Cash budget
A schedule forecasting of cash inflows and cash outflows over a specified period.

Cash flow
This term may have different meanings, depending upon who is using the term and in what context. Bankers usually define it as net profit plus all noncash expenses (depreciation and amortization), but it can also be defined as the difference between cash receipts and disbursements over a specified period. This text describes operating cash flow and financing cash flow, which differ slightly from the definitions applied by a CPA in their statement of cash flow as provided with CPA-prepared financial statements.

Collateral
Assets that secure a loan.

Common-sized balance sheet or income statement
The process of dividing individual revenue and expense account balances by total revenue or dividing an individual asset, liability, or equity account by total assets to determine each account's value as a percentage of revenue or total assets. For the balance sheet, each account is divided by total assets. For the income statement, each account is divided by revenue.

Comprehensive financial plan
A comprehensive financial plan is comprised of a historical review and a three-year forecast of the income statement, balance sheet, cash flow, and financial ratios.

Contribution margin

The difference between revenue and variable expenses:

Revenue	$400,000
Minus variable expenses	(150,000)
Contribution margin	250,000

This tells you that you have $250,000 left after paying variable expenses to pay fixed expenses. If your fixed expenses exceed $250,000, then you need to either increase revenue or reduce fixed expenses, or both, to avoid losing money.

Contribution margin ratio (CMR)

The contribution margin expressed as a percentage of revenue.
contribution margin ÷ revenue = contribution margin ratio.

Corporation

A type of business organization chartered by a state and given legal rights as a separate entity. A C corporation is a tax-paying entity, and an S corporation is not a tax-paying entity but passes its profits (or losses) through to its shareholders.

Cost of goods sold

Expenses related directly to the production of revenue for a business. This usually includes raw materials, direct labor, freight, and factory overhead for a manufacturing company; merchandise costs for a wholesaler or retailer; and direct labor and materials for a service company. This is also referred to as direct expenses for a service company.

Current assets

Current assets are those assets of a company that are reasonably expected to be converted to cash or consumed during the next twelve months from the date of the balance sheet. Current assets include cash, accounts receivable, inventories, and prepaid expenses (note that accounts receivable and prepaid expenses exist only on an accrual-basis balance sheet).

Current liabilities

Liabilities that are due within twelve months of the date of the balance sheet. Current liabilities include such accounts as a bank line of credit, accrued liabilities, accounts payable, and current portion of long-term debt (note that accounts payable and accrued expenses exist only on an accrual-basis balance sheet).

Current ratio

This ratio is a measure of liquidity and the company's ability to pay its bills. It is calculated by dividing current assets by current liabilities.

Debt-to-equity ratio

This ratio is a measure of the company's safety and ability to survive adversity. It is calculated by dividing total liabilities by equity. This is an important ratio for banks since it is one way to measure a company's risk level.

Depreciation expense

The amount of expense a company charges against earnings to write off the cost of fixed assets over their useful lives. If the expense is assumed to be incurred in equal amounts in each business period over the life of the asset, the depreciation method used is straight line (SL). If the expense is assumed to be front-loaded and incurred in decreasing amounts in each business period over the life of the asset, the method used is accelerated. Straight-line depreciation is chosen for financial statement purposes, and accelerated depreciation is chosen for tax return purposes. This produces a lower profit on the tax return and is permitted by IRS regulations.

Direct expenses

This is the same as the cost of goods sold. Usually used in reference to a service type business.

Dividend

That portion of a corporation's earnings that is paid to the stockholders and not retained in the business.

Entrepreneur

A person who assumes the risk of starting a business.

Equity

The net worth or ownership interest in a company. It is the difference between the assets and the liabilities of a company. In a corporation, net worth or owner's equity consists of capital stock, capital surplus, and retained earnings.

Financial gap

The financial gap represents the amount of funding the business is unable to generate internally to purchase the assets required to support revenue. The business must make up the difference with either debt or additional equity.

Fixed assets

Those assets of a noncurrent nature, which will not normally be converted into cash during the next twelve months (which are current assets). Examples are furniture and fixtures, land, buildings, and equipment. A fixed asset that is to be sold within twelve months is not considered to be a current asset.

Fixed expenses

Those expenses that do not vary directly with revenue. Examples include rent, depreciation, lease expense, office expenses, legal, and accounting.

Fluctuating current assets

Those assets that go up and down with seasonal fluctuations in revenue. Typically, they are the seasonal demands for inventory and accounts receivable.

Goodwill

Goodwill is an intangible asset that is created to the extent that the purchase price of a company is greater than the fair market value of the total assets. It is synonymous with the term blue sky, and it can only arise on a balance sheet as the result of purchasing a business. Treatment of goodwill for tax or accounting purposes changes from time to time, and it is therefore necessary to ask your CPA how it should be handled.

Gross profit

The difference between revenue and the cost of goods sold.

$1,500,000	revenue
($975,000)	minus cost of goods sold (direct expenses)
$525,000	equals gross profit

This tells you that you have $525,000 in gross profit to pay overhead or indirect expenses. If your overhead exceeds $525,000, then you either need to increase your gross profit margin, reduce overhead, or both.

Gross profit margin (GPM)

The gross profit expressed as a percentage of revenue.
Revenue ÷ gross profit = gross profit margin
A gross profit margin of 35 percent would mean that there is $0.35 in gross profit for every $1.00 in revenue.

Income statement

The statement of revenue, expenses, and profit for a particular period. It is known as a period statement. Also referred to as the Profit & Loss statement or the P&L.

Indirect expense

Same as operating expense, general and administrative expense (G&A) or overhead. Usually used in reference to a service-type business.

Intangible assets

Nonphysical assets such as goodwill, patents, copyrights, operating authorities, and trademarks. These assets are routinely subtracted from total assets and equity by the banker for analysis purposes.

Inventory turnover

The number of times a business turns its inventory over during the year. This is calculated by dividing the cost of goods sold by inventory.

Liabilities

Amounts owed to creditors by a person or a business.

Limited liability company (LLC)

A form of business, similar to a corporation, with liability protection for all of the owners (referred to as members). It is taxed in the same fashion as an S corporation.

Line of credit

An agreement whereby a bank agrees to lend a customer funds up to the agreed maximum amount. A line of credit is typically used for seasonal needs to finance inventory and accounts receivable and is secured by accounts receivable that do not exceed ninety days.

Liquidity

A term to describe a firm's ability to meet its current obligations. It is measured by the current ratio.

Long-term debt

Liabilities that are due more than one year from the date of the balance sheet.

Markup

The difference between the cost and selling prices of merchandise, usually expressed as a percentage. To calculate markup as a percentage, use the difference between the cost and selling prices for the numerator and the cost for the denominator. An item that cost $1.00 and had a selling price of $1.50 would have a 50 percent markup ($0.50 ÷ $1.00). This is not the same as but is often confused with, the gross profit margin. In the above example, the gross profit margin would be thirty-three percent (.50 ÷ 1.50). Markup is applied to the cost, and gross profit margin is applied to the sales price.

Mortgage

A long-term debt with real estate pledged as collateral.

Net income

Often used by CPAs to signify net profit after tax.

Net loss

The excess of total expenses over total income for a fiscal period, either before or after-tax.

Net present value (NPV)

The net present value is equal to the present value of future returns, minus the present value of future payments.

Net profit

The excess of total income over the total expenses for a fiscal period, before income taxes.

Net profit margin

The net profit (before tax) as expressed as a percentage of revenue. Net profit ÷ revenue equals net profit margin.

Note payable
A written promise to a person or business to pay a certain amount at a certain time.

Operating cash flow
The cash flow the company generates from its day-to-day operations. The description of operating cash flow in chapter four is slightly different from the one provided by a CPA-prepared statement of cash flow.

Operating expenses
Those expenses pertaining to the normal operation of the business. Interest expense and nonrecurring losses are not included as operating expenses. Also referred to as overhead or indirect expense.

Operating profit
The difference between the gross profit and overhead or indirect expenses. This tells you the amount of profit that has been generated from operations of your business.

Revenue	$950,000
Cost of goods sold	(500,000)
Gross profit	450,000
Overhead expenses	(400,000)
Operating profit	50,000

Operating profit margin
The operating profit expressed as a percentage of revenue.
Operating profit ÷ revenue equals operating profit margin (OPM).
50,000 ÷ 950,000 = 5.3%

Permanent current assets
Represents the permanent base of current assets (inventory, accounts receivable, and cash) that a business will have on hand based on the revenue level of the business at its lowest period. In other words, current assets do not go down to zero, and the lowest amount during the year represents the amount of permanent current assets that the business will have.

Preferred stock

The stock that grants its owners certain preference rights over common stockholders, usually dividend and voting rights.

Present value

The value today of a future receipt or payment of money discounted at an appropriate discount rate. The present value of an amount to be received in the future is worth less than the future face amount because of the need to wait for the payment, thus preventing you from earning any return (like interest) on it. Receiving $1.00 in one year's time is the same as a present value of $0.95 if it is discounted at 5 percent. In other words, if you had $0.95 today, it would be worth $1.00 in a year if it were invested at 5 percent. Net present value is the difference between the present value of future receipts and the present value of future payments.

Quick assets

Cash, accounts receivable, and marketable securities.

Quick ratio

The quick ratio is calculated by dividing quick assets by current liabilities. This ratio is not typically calculated for service businesses because it will be very like the current ratio.

Retained earnings

Earnings of the business that have been retained in the business and not paid out to stockholders.

Return on assets (ROA)

Return on assets is the ratio of net profit (before taxes) to total assets.
Net profit ÷ total assets = return on assets

Return on equity (ROE)

Return on equity is the ratio of net profit (before taxes) to equity or net worth. This may also be referred to as return on investment (ROI).
Net profit ÷ equity = return on equity

Revenue
Synonymous with sales.

Sales to assets ratio
This is the ratio of sales or revenue divided by total assets.
Sales ÷ total assets = sales to assets ratio

Sales to net fixed assets ratio
This is the ratio of sales or revenue divided by net fixed assets.
Sales ÷ net fixed assets = sales to net fixed assets ratio

Secured loan
A loan that is secured by some collateral, as opposed to an unsecured loan. Secured loans may be either long-term or short-term loans.

Self-liquidating loan
A short-term commercial loan, usually supported by a lien on a given product or commodity, which is liquidated from the proceeds of the sale of the product or commodity.

Stockholder
A person owning shares of the capital stock of a corporation. Also referred to as a shareholder.

Term loan
A long-term loan due in more than one year.

Trend analysis
The process of measuring financial data over a given period to note any significant changes in performance from period to period.

Variable assets
Those assets that go up or down with sales or revenue volume, such as accounts receivable. These assets are needed to support revenue.

Variable expenses
Expenses that are caused by revenue and go up or down with sales or revenue volume. Examples include commissions, direct wages, supplies, and bad debts.

Variable liabilities

Those liabilities that go up or down with revenue volume. They typically are accounts payable and accrued expenses.

Working capital

This is defined as current assets minus current liabilities. All financially stable companies need adequate working capital so that they can make payments when they are due, either to vendors, employees, or creditors. A current ratio of 2.00 means that there is $2.00 in current assets to pay every $1.00 in current liabilities, or $1.00 in working capital ($2.00 minus $1.00).

BIBLIOGRAPHY

Arrendondo, Lani, *Communicating Effectively*, McGraw-Hill, 2000.

Covey, Stephen, *Principled-Centered Leadership*, Simon & Schuster, 1992.

Cross, Dick, *60-Minute CEO: Mastering Leadership an Hour at a Time*, Bibliomotion, Inc., 2014

Duryee, David A., *60 Minute CFO: The Fast Track to Understanding Finance for Movers*, 2017.

Duryee, David A., *The Business Owner's Guide to Achieving Financial Success*, Richard D. Irwin, Inc., 1994.

Gerber, Michael E., *The E Myth Revisited*, Harper Collins, Inc. 1995.

Hoffman, Bryce, *American Icon: Alan Mulally and the Fight to Save Ford Motor Company*, Crown Publishing Group, 2012.

Isaacson, Walter, *Steve Jobs*, Simon & Shuster, 2011.

Le Van, Gerald, *The Survival Guide for Business Families*, Rutledge, 1999.

Julien, Scott M., *What Every Leader Needs to Know: 7 Essential Leadership Secrets*, printed by CreateSpace, an Amazon.com company, 2009.

Posner, Barry, Kouzes, James, *The Leadership Challenge*, Jossey Bass, 1997.

Stack, Jack, *The Great Game of Business*, Bantam Doubleday Dell Publishing Group, Inc. 1992.

ACKNOWLEDGMENTS

I would be remiss if I did not acknowledge and thank the dozens of CEO's who have freely shared their information and knowledge with me over the last thirty-five years and allowed me to enjoy an intimate look at their operations. Because of this, I have developed valuable insights into the leadership qualities of successful business owners. It has been a rich and enjoyable learning experience for me.

I have the utmost admiration and respect for business owners who are students of the game and strive every day to learn and grow and be better in their roles as CEOs and business leaders. Being a good leader is tough and demanding, and only those that diligently work at it and follow the tenets of this book are the ones who consistently excel.

A special thanks to those that helped me so much with the planning, editing, and design of this book. Allen Hopson designed and developed the workbooks that are available for this book. Claudeen Lyle, Sabrina Jones, Kevin St. George, Brandt Allen, John Colosimo, Chuck Feinstein, Art King, and Allen Hopson spent many hours going over this manuscript and provided me with invaluable corrections, suggestions, and insights. My daughter, Tracy Bech, designed the website, and Christin Dunbar designed the cover, and I am very grateful for their help.

You all have made this a much better book, and I am truly indebted to you all.

AUTHOR'S NOTE

Julian and Allen are real people, as are their wives, Sara and Debbie. They are father and son and have graciously agreed to use their names in this book. Julian did retire to Florida and passed on the business to Allen as the successor CEO.

The rest of the story, however, is fiction. Allen managed the company just like dad, in a careful, effective, profitable manner, and with great integrity.

My narrative regarding Durson Distributors is not all fictitious, however. It is a composite of many companies that I have observed over the years. Conflicts between generations are inevitable, and it is not easy to pass a business successfully on to the next generation, and few do. Conservative mom and dad are bound to clash with hard-charging son or daughter on the best course of action for the business. The goal of them all should be to get into the thunder phase of business *and stay there.*

It is easier said than done. Good communication and careful attention to the tenets of this book are the keys to making it happen.

Success isn't predestined; it is earned. Leaders are not born; they are made. If you give these principles 60 minutes a month, you and your leadership team will have a solid chance to be financially successful and stay in the Thunder Phase of business.

ABOUT THE AUTHOR

David A. Duryee is the managing director of Horizon Management Services LLC and has been active in business consulting, succession planning and financial training for over forty years. He received his BA and MBA in finance from the University of Washington and is an honors graduate of the Pacific Coast Banking School. He was a banker for sixteen years, serving initially as a commercial lending officer and subsequently as Vice President and Manager of Corporate Management Services in the Trust Division. In 1980 he co-founded and operated a consulting firm that subsequently merged with a major accounting firm where he served as manager of Valuation Services in the consulting division.

In addition to this book, Mr. Duryee is the author or co-author of several books, including *60 Minute CFO: The fast track to understanding finance for movers; The Business Owner's Guide to Achieving Financial Success; A Dealer Guide to Financial Management;* and *Small Business Banking, Assessing Needs and Establishing Strategies,* as well as numerous articles in trade publications. He is a nationally known lecturer to business owners, bankers, and professionals and sits on several corporations' advisory boards.

Mr. Duryee served in the U.S. Army, achieving the rank of Captain as an artillery battery commander, and was awarded the Army Commendation Medal for outstanding leadership.

Mr. Duryee divides his time between Austin, Texas, and Hood River, Oregon, with his wife of over fifty years, Anne.

Reach him at dave@60minutecfo.com. Download complimentary Excel-based workbooks for this book from www.60minutecfo.com.

BOOK REVIEW

If you liked this book, please take a moment and go to Amazon and give it a review.

https://www.amazon.com/60-Minute-CFO-Bridging-Business-ebook/dp/B073R1DKKJ/ref=sr_1_1?ie=UTF8&qid=1545949717&sr=8-1&keywords=60+minute+cfo

All suggestions on how to improve it or make concepts more understandable, including grammar or typos, are most welcome. I appreciate your feedback!

Please contact me at dave@60minutecfo.com with any comments.

Thank you and keep on paddling!

CPSIA information can be obtained
at www.ICGtesting.com
Printed in the USA
LVHW021558250521
688467LV00008B/781